Spread the Fed

"Hockett has, for years, proven unique in his ability to fuse the legal, economic and financial codes and histories of the world—and particularly of the United States—into a cohesive, rigorously interdisciplinary narrative. His years of studying and working within the U.S. Federal Reserve System have yielded this masterful insight on how the U.S. central banking system slowly abandoned its charge to enable and accelerate the commercial development of all regions of the nation, in favor of the Fed's becoming the steward of global financialization. Hockett's argument—to refocus the Fed on its original productive mission—offers not only improved domestic economic outcomes, but a resulting solution to regional and political divisions that threaten America... and have now come to destabilize the world."

—Daniel Alpert, *Founding and Managing Partner, Westwood Capital LLC and author of* The Age of Oversupply

"Don't be fooled by this book's title. It is about far more than the US Federal Reserve system (though it is quite good at explaining that). It is also a brilliant dissection of long-festering flaws in our economic system that: elevate speculation over productive investment, fail to stabilize prices, and no longer promote a secure middle class. Best of all, it shows how relatively modest changes in the operation of the Fed could go a long way toward fixing these and other flaws. Highly recommended for policymakers in the new Administration and elsewhere."

—Peter Barnes, *entrepreneur and author of* With Liberty and Dividends for All

"Robert Hockett uncovers the politics and policy behind the mysterious institutional design of the Federal Reserve, and shows how concentrated financial power undid the regulated, distributed, balanced growth-and-development model that the Fed was built to foster. With the verve and authority that is his trademark, he calls for renewing that mission—to rebuild, reindustrialize, de-financialize, decentralize, and so to restore dynamism with decency to American life."

—James K. Galbraith, *Lloyd M. Bentsen Jr. Chair in Government/Business Relations and Professor of Government, The University of Texas at Austin*

"Hockett's book is a lucid and engaging tale about the history of the US Federal Reserve and how the institution might be re-imagined to better steer the direction of economic growth, helping to mitigate the biggest crises of our time, from climate change to rising inequality."

—Mariana Mazzucato, *Professor in Economics of Innovation and Public Value + Founding Director of the Institute for Innovation and Public Purpose, University College London and author of* Mission Economy

"Spread the Fed is a must-read for policymakers, economists, and anyone interested in the future of central banking. The book contributes significantly to the ongoing debate about the role of central banks in the 21st century. Hockett's vision of a decentralized, democratized Federal Reserve is not just a theoretical exercise; it offers a pragmatic blueprint focused on ensuring a more equitable and resilient economy."

—Julia M. Puaschunder, *Postdoctoral Scientist, Interuniversity Consortium of New York, Columbia University and author of* The Future of Resilient Finance

"Banking in the US used to be legally required to be small-scale and local in orientation. That, in turn, assured (a) productive 'patient capital' investment rather than destructively speculative financialization, (b) reasonably even development across all of our nation's many diverse regions, and (c) long-term financial and monetary stability. As Robert Hockett of Cornell University and previously the New York Fed shows, a key part of this better arrangement was what he calls the original Federal Reserve System's 'distributed' structure and associated regional-productivist orientation. By bringing this original system back—through the process of what he calls 'spreading the Fed'—Hockett shows, we can restore sustainably and democratically productive, not speculative, human development back to our nation as well as to the wider world."

—Susan Witt, *Cofounder, BerkShares Community Currency and Executive Director, Schumaker Center for a New Economics*

Robert C. Hockett

Spread the Fed

Distributed Central Banking for Productive-Republican Finance

palgrave
macmillan

Robert C. Hockett
Cornell University
Ithaca, NY, USA

ISBN 978-3-031-72050-5 ISBN 978-3-031-72051-2 (eBook)
https://doi.org/10.1007/978-3-031-72051-2

This Palgrave Macmillan imprint is published by the registered company Springer Nature Switzerland AG
The registered company address is: Gewerbestrasse 11, 6330 Cham, Switzerland

Acknowledgements

Among the living, I heartily thank my 'brother' Dan Alpert, Peter Barnes, Kaushik Basu, Lawrence Baxter, my 'sister' Sarah Bloom Raskin, Mark Blyth, my 'everything' Blanca Braun, Partha Dasgupta, Jeni Dhodary, my 'sister' Rana Foroohar, my pal Jamie Galbraith, my 'brother' Aaron James, Roberto Mangabeira Unger, my 'sister' Marianna Mazzucato, my 'brother' Paul McCulley, Fred Moseley, Martin O'Neil, Julia Puaschunder, my mentor John Roemer, my mentor Robert Shiller, Alan Thomas, Michael Thompson, and Susan Witt. I owe a particularly strong debt to Bronwyn Geyer and her superb colleagues at Palgrave Macmillan.

Among those who have left us, I wish that I could directly thank Preffor G.A. Cohen, Professor Enrique Dussel, Senator Carter Glass, Treasury Secretary Alexander Hamilton, Finanzminister Rudolf Hilferding, H.M. Treasury Minister-without-Portfolio J.M. Keynes, Controller General John Law, Ms. Rosa Luxemburg, Herr Doktor Karl Marx, Ministre des Finances Jacques Necker, Sir James Steuart, Mr. Henry Thornton, Professor Léon Walras, Mr. Paul Warburg, Professor Knut Wicksell, and the recently departed Professor Erik Olin Wright.

Introduction

Abstract This Introduction to the full Book explains the Book's motivation, goals, and plan of approach, while also 'road-mapping' the argument unfolded over the subsequent chapters. The Book's guiding normative ideals, it explains, are those of what it calls 'Productive Republicanism' and 'Productivist Central Banking' as the essential organ through which Productive-Republicanism is vindicated in the realm of national credit and monetary policy. The historical narrative that the Book narrates, in turn, this Introduction describes as that of a nation committed both to the Productive Republican ideal and to Productivist Central Banking, albeit with a certain distinctively American ambivalence over the 'centrality' involved in all central banking owing to America's not altogether felicitous history with colonial British governance. That ambivalence, along with the diversity of America's continent-spanning economy, led to what the Book calls 'central banking with federalist characteristics.' Finally, the Introduction makes plain, the U.S. lost sight of Productive Republicanism and Productivist Central Banking alike in the second half of the twentieth century, necessitating the present Book's 'restorative reform' plan for a revitalized Productivist Federal Reserve System operating through all twelve of its dispersed regional District Banks.

Keywords Allocation, Bank Money, Banking, Central Banking, Commodity Markets, Commodity Reserves, Credit-Money, Crude RBD, Deflation, Elastic Currency, Fed, Federalism, Federal Reserve District Banks, Federal Reserve System, Federalism, Fisher, Inflation,

Interest Rates, Law, Marx, Modulation, Money, Money Markets, New Deal, OMO, OPEC, Open Market Operations, Production, Productivism, Productivist Central Banking, Productive-Republicanism, RBD, Real Bills Doctrine, Recursive Collective Action Problems, Refined RBD, Rehypothecation, Republicanism, SIPIs, Smith, Speculation, Steuart, Strategic Reserves, Strong-Form RBD, Systemically Important Prices & Indices, QE, Quantitative Easing, Thornton, Walras, Weak-Form RBD, Wicksell.

This book consolidates and synthesizes, into one integrated narrative and resultant comprehensive plan of action, work that I have been doing both inside and outside of the Federal Reserve System ('FRS,' 'the Fed') on its history, its purposes, and its still scarcely tapped potential for over a decade. The Book's central argument combines a positive history with a normative plan of what it calls 'restorative' Fed renewal—a renewal, perhaps surprisingly, largely rooted in the institution's original purposes and early practices. I call the upshot a (re-)—that is, a once again—'distributed' Fed: a Fed that is once again operative across regions and markets in need of both liquid capital and price stability, as envisaged by its founders and practiced by its staff in its early decades in keeping with what I call longstanding American Productive-Republican normative ideals.[1]

Positively, the book shows that the Federal Reserve System was sensibly founded, like the then-contemporaneous German banking model that partly inspired it, to function as a cross-regional network of industrial development finance institutions. This network was tasked with enabling uninterrupted, perpetually productive industrial growth across all twelve of our country's diverse regional economies by ensuring both (a) a stable supply of liquidity and bank credit money and (b) markets insulated from all forms of volatility not rooted in genuine fundamentals as distinguished from ephemeral 'swings' stemming from what I long ago identified as what I call 'Recursive Collective Action Problems' ('ReCAPS' for short) and related market failures.[2]

Normatively, the book then shows both (a) why this original Productive-Republican Fed must, and (b) how it indeed can, be restored in an updated, twenty-first-century rendition. The resultant reconstruction, we'll find, builds on and 'modernizes' the prior construction, of whose original purpose and wisdom we've gradually lost sight as a nation over the past half-century or more. And while the history I shall relate and draw lessons from is American, much of what's here can be generalized to other jurisdictions—from many of which the Fed's founders took lessons in designing our own nation's first modern central bank.

The mentioned original form the Fed took was, I argue, the *only* form in which U.S. popular opinion, which had been acutely ambivalent about when not actively hostile to concentrated financial power, the dangers of unproductive speculation, and hence central banking itself since the earliest days of the Republic, could accept anything resembling a then-European style central bank for the U.S. The requisite form was thus a partly decentralized, public/private and local/national *hybrid* form, even while taking on just so much centralization and public sector authority as was necessary to ensure both cross-regional and cross-temporal coordination and uniformity on the part of the currency whose administration was moved from the Treasury to the new central bank.

That hybrid form *also*, I argue, is not accidentally the *only* form now compatible with a materially productive and equitably prosperous, rather than a merely speculative, financialized, deindustrialized, and inequitably class-riven American economy of the sort that's developed and plagued us in recent decades. It is, in other words, the only form compatible with what I call the U.S.' 'Productive Republican' heritage—a form I'll call by turns 'Productivist' and 'Productive-Republican' central banking.

This hybrid form of central banking and monetary administration upon which the Fed's bipartisan and geographically diverse founders and Congressional supporters settled in 1913, modeled in part upon then-rapidly-growing Germany's 'discount' industrial banking system,[3] was a triumph of theoretically well-informed practical compromise. It enabled both the public and private sectors, and both federal and local entities, to do precisely what each can do best in a broadly opportunity-egalitarian democratic partnership of the kind that's entailed by Productive Republicanism. It housed cross-regional coordination, continent- and market-spanning macroeconomic oversight, and currency-issuance authority at the federal level, while housing productive-project selection and execution responsibilities at the local and private sector levels.

The upshot of this unique public/private, federal/local partnership arrangement was a specifically American rendition of the aforementioned (and still successfully functioning!) German 'discount system.' This was a system whereby regional Federal Reserve District Banks issued new currency (to this day called 'Federal Reserve Notes') and its bank credit equivalent (what Wicksell in the late nineteenth century dubbed 'bank-money,' later rechristened 'credit-money') in exchange for short-term debt ('commercial paper') issued by businesses to finance Fed-criteria-conforming productive (not speculative) business start-up and expansion plans. It was everything that one could hope for: a flexibly stable—in bank parlance, 'elastic'—money supply for productive (not speculative) industrial growth across every distinct region and market of our diverse transcontinental economy.

New money was issued, in other words, in amounts no more and no less than required to finance new *production* (not speculation)—that is, the very goods and services that would *absorb* all new money thus issued. This meant, at least in conjunction with other measures that we shall be mapping below, both no inflation and no deflation—a 'Goldilocks' credit-money supply, as it were, to accommodate all potential new production and nothing more (no mere speculation).

Tragically, however, a single correctible intellectual error embedded within the Fed's founding monetary theory and associated execution of functions led to its mishandling the late 'Roaring 20s' asset price bubble—in essence, a hyperinflation—and the ensuing Great Crash of 1929 and Fisher-style debt-deflation ('Great Depression') of the early 1930s. (The gold standard, still operative then, of course worsened the problem in ways we shall see.) The inverse of this error, which was equally erroneous 'from the opposite direction,' as it were, unfortunately then led *Congress* to *misdiagnose* what had gone wrong and thus rewrite the Fed's mandate in a symmetrically problematic way by 1935.

This rewrite, alas, was just as mistaken—again, from the 'opposite direction'—as were the Fed's responses to the bubble and bust of the late 1920s and early 1930s. The result, with which we still live in worsened form for reasons laid out below, is a Federal Reserve System now needlessly far removed from its original purpose. Indeed it is *so* far removed that its original designers, the brilliant Paul Warburg and Carter Glass (now better known for the Glass-Steagall Act), would likely be 'rolling' in their proverbial 'graves' were they here to see it. So would our nation's Federalist founders, who would have approved the 1913 Fed but likely not the current Fed.

From a regionally distributed national network of 'Main Street' industrial development bank adjuncts, our central bank has morphed into a DC/NYC-centric and 'Wall Street'-focused money-pump that encourages, aids, and abets destructive and wealth-destroying and -concentrating speculation and 'financialization' rather than wealth-generating and wealth-spreading productive development. It thus brings regular devastating price inflations and deflations rather than stably and steadily growing production and broadly distributed material prosperity as originally and providentially intended and effected by the 1913 Fed.

Departing as they did from the Fed's original founding mission, the Fed reforms of the 1930s also have left us with twelve distinct regional District Banks whose purpose, once obvious and warmly embraced by productive American businesses, local banks, and citizens more broadly, is now obscure not only to most Americans, but even to many Fed personnel (my former colleagues) themselves. Most Americans who attend to such matters now effectively and not inaccurately see the Fed District Banks as little more than regional data-aggregators and 'think tanks'—helpful roles, to be sure, but a far cry from what was originally intended and done, not to mention from what is still sorely needed.

If all of Fed policymaking and functionality are now concentrated in the Board and the Federal Open Market Committee in Washington and the New York Fed trading desk in Manhattan, many accordingly now ask, why do we have regional Federal Reserve District Banks in Chicago, St. Louis, Kansas City, Dallas, Atlanta, etc. *at all*?

The principal answer, we'll see, is that these are all vestiges of the Fed's original purpose, which now both can and must be made *functional* again by making the Fed *productive* again—in an updated rendition of its original and in-the-main well-conceived mandate. All we need do is respond *soundly* to the aforementioned intellectual error of 1913, rather than continuing to make the same mistake 'in reverse' as Congress did in 1935 and as we all have done, in effect, as a polity ever since.

So what *is* this 'intellectual error' to which I refer above, which brought on the oddly vestigial Fed we now live with? This is where the 'theoretical' contributions made by the book and *also* mentioned above come into play. In a phrase, the intellectual error to which I allude is a particular rendition—a tragically *incomplete* rendition—of the readily refined and hence ultimately potentially sound 'Real Bills Doctrine' ('RBD') upon which the Fed at its founding was founded.

The RBD as understood in 1913 viewed all money as endogenously generated spendable credit—in essence, Fed credit-money issued to 'monetize,' through purchase, commercial paper (short-term debt instruments) issued by businesses in connection with productive projects as described above.[4] Tying Fed credit-money issuance to all and only production-associated commercial paper issued by producing firms, it was widely believed, would guarantee money supplies neither too large nor too small. This would be true, it was thought, irrespective of whether the Fed purchased such paper directly from issuing firms or from Federal Reserve Member Banks that had themselves done so.[5]

What I shall lay out below as what I call sound money *allocation* across multiple regional industries and firms for all and only such projects as promised *production* (not merely profits[6]), in other words, was considered both *necessary and sufficient* to vouchsafe what below I'll lay out as what I have long labeled sound money *modulation* — i.e., monetary aggregates neither too large (hence inflationary) nor too small (hence deflationary)—economy-wide.[7] Smart *allocation* of new credit-money always and everywhere only for productive (not merely profitable) projects across the economy, it was thought, would prevent both inflationary over-issuance and deflationary under-issuance of new credit-money by the Fed, hence would assure optimal money supply *modulation* .

Insofar as Fed credit-money supplies *are* endogenously generated and issued in response only to production plans whose produced goods or services could absorb all new money,[8] this view was perfectly sound. And the Fed as then constituted was accordingly also in large part well-founded. The problem, however, is that the money supply at any given time is *not* only endogenously generated to finance solely productive projects—and even when it *is* thus originally generated, safeguards are needed to prevent what I shall call unproductive '*re*-generation' *ad libitum* via what I shall call 'rehypothecation risk.'

Money can *also*, in short, be (a) endogenously *over*-generated in support of *non*-productive, merely *speculative* (even while profitable[9]) 'projects' that do not produce means of absorbing new money, or (b) *exogenously* grown or shrunken by sudden inflows or outflows of money from 'outside' the ordinarily operating system—such as German war reparations and Allied debt payments (largely in gold) after the First World War, for example, which helped fuel the Wall Street speculation of the later 1920s, or the OPEC-engineered oil price 'shock' of the 1970s, which affected what below I introduce as a 'Systemically Important Price or Index' ('SIPI') to similar effect.[10]

The old 1913 understanding of the RBD, making inadequate provision for such possibilities as (a) and (b) just mentioned, thus blinded both Fed and Congressional leaders alike to two critical sources of possible monetary disturbance unaddressed by issuing Fed money even when only in initial connection with productive business start-up or expansion plans. The 1913 understanding of the RBD was in this sense precisely half true: RBD-style initial Fed money allocation solely to productive projects was *necessary* for the sound allocation and modulation of monetary aggregates, but was not of itself *sufficient* to that end.

Congress's *reaction* to the error was accordingly *also* half right—it simply got right what the 1913 framers had got wrong, *while* getting *wrong* what the 1913 framers had got *right*. Altogether abjuring Fed credit-money allocation, which it now viewed as unnecessary to sound modulation, and establishing a new Federal Open Market Committee ('FOMC') to work directly on aggregate modulation alone, which *it* now mistakenly took for sufficient to get monetary aggregates right, the 1935 Congress in effect left us with the 'photographic negative' of what the Congress of 1913 had wrought.

The new understanding post-1935, in other words, was equally incomplete to that of 1913, but incomplete 'from the opposite side' of the necessary pairing of sound allocation of endogenous money *and* sound modulation of both endogenous and *exogenous* money.

In short, then, effective—that is, productive (not merely profitable)—allocation is necessary, but is not sufficient, to vouchsafe effective modulation. The latter requires adequate FOMC-style counteracting of exogenously sourced influxes and effluxes of money alongside 1913-style monetization of endogenously issued commercial paper sold in connection with all and only such business startup or expansion projects as promise expanded *production*. The still Productive-Republican-minded Congress of 1913 caught the necessity but missed the non-*sufficiency* piece of this fuller picture, while the 1935 Congress, which we'll see first relocated allocation authority to brand new Deal agencies (one of which, significantly, used the Fed District Banks as offices) rather than to the Fed and then abjured allocation altogether, in the long term effectively forgot the *necessity* piece of the same.

What is accordingly needed now is a recovery and retention, respectively, of what both the 1913 and 1935 Congresses got right, without what those Congresses got wrong. It is necessary, in other words, that we restore full regionally distributed productive Fed 'discounting' of productive commercial paper—*not* exclusively modulation-focused Quantitative Easing ('QE') for speculative Wall Street megabanks—as the Fed's principal form of new-money-issuance, while *ending non-productive* such issuance and *sterilizing exogenously* sourced money *influxes and effluxes*. This will be, in effect, to act upon a refining reformulation of the old Real Bills Doctrine—what I will call 'Refined,' or 'Weak-Form' RBD.

In addition, and perhaps ironically, it turns out that even direct Fed *modulatory* activity must now be 'spread,' as I am putting it here, to markets additional to those in which it is currently operative. For money rental prices—'interest rates'—are no longer the sole Systemically Important Prices and Indices (again, 'SIPIs') with which we must now be collectively concerned. As recent events have demonstrated, there are other prices subject to non-'fundamentals'-based price swings that tend in turn to affect other prices that concern us all. I allude in particular to fuel, food, and other commodity prices that fluctuate in amplitudes far beyond what 'fundamentals' explain—and wreak havoc on the stability of other prices, in view of their systemic significance, as well.

Hence the renewal of a 'distributed' Fed that I design and advocate here includes not only a (re-) distribution across geographical regions, but also across several key markets beyond the money markets in which the Fed presently conducts open market operations ('OMO'). And while the renewed focus on productive *allocation* will take care of *much* of this new modulatory need by itself, additional *direct* modulatory attention will likely be needed—through means analogous to those the Fed already employs in the money market, as I'll lay out near the end of the book. (In short, the Fed will have to act on certain commodity markets through Chicago Fed OMO just as it long has done in the money markets through New York Fed OMO.)

This, then, is the 'restorative renewal' or 'renewing restoration' that I ultimately advocate and show how to effectuate in the Chapters below. Here then is how we'll proceed ...

Part I starts us off with a brief history of American money, credit, and credit-money—their issuance, dissemination, and management. The focus is first on the nation's reluctant and hence gradual path toward real central banking and monetary management, then on its first modern and now contemporary attempts to vest central bank functions with the regionally distributed, Productive-Republican-and Federalist-inspired Federal Reserve System established in 1913.

Chapter 1 sets the stage by recounting America's troubled history with central banking from the Founding Era to 1913. In particular, it shows how our historical oscillations between favoring central banking and disfavoring it parallel the American polity's broader oscillations between favoring federal and public sector capacity on the one hand, state and private sector prerogatives on the other—that is, the well-known Federalist/Antifederalist dialectic of American history that continues to unfold to this day.

It is no accident, we find, that Alexander Hamilton's First Bank of the U.S., which functioned as a combined money-allocating central and industry-promoting national development bank, coincided with the ascendancy of the Federalists—including George Washington and his Treasury Secretary Hamilton—and the new centralizing Constitution that they promulgated to replace the original (and inoperable) Articles of Confederation. Nor is it an accident that our first experiment with something like central banking then ended with the ascendancy to the White House of our most militantly *anti*-Federalist President to date at that point, Andrew Jackson.

It is also no accident, this Chapter indicates, that the first *still-enduring* establishment of federal supremacy over matters monetary comes with the *Civil War*, which both settled the question of federal supremacy in our constitutional order once and for all, *and* bequeathed us the national banking system, the national bank chartering authority and activity regulator (the Office of the Comptroller of the Currency ('OCC') still within Treasury), and the currency (the 'greenback' dollar bill) that we use to this day notwithstanding our subsequent relocation of its issuance to the Fed once we founded it.

Our monetary and central banking dialectic, the chapter concludes, just is our federal versus state and our public versus private dialectics as refracted in the realm of finance.

Chapter 2 then turns to the Fed specifically—both its founding and its early 'operating system.' Here the emphasis is on how we at last came to find central banking unavoidable in a modern, industrial economy on the one hand, while having to satisfy that need via what I call 'central banking with federalist characteristics' on the other. The characteristics I emphasize are a *'distributed,' federated structure*—'decentralization'—on the one hand, and a favoring of 'Main Street' *production* over 'Wall Street' *speculation* on the other. This in turn meant both significant regional autonomy on the one hand, and influence by local industries and the mandatorily localized banks that financed them on the other hand.

Most of the American Founders, Chapter 2 finds in a partial echo of Chapter 1's themes, had been heavily indebted to speculative London banks during the colonial era, and had accordingly developed a healthy suspicion both of concentrated monetary authority such as had been practiced from London, and of 'high finance' as a realm of 'gambling and stock-jobbing' rather than bona fide productive lending. That suspicion, born of hard experience, became part of our nation's financial culture from the very beginning, and has been reflected in much of our law ever since. The Federal Reserve Act of 1913 fell squarely within that tradition—what I am calling the Productive-Republican tradition conceived in contrast to eighteenth-century British financial aristocracy.

Happily, we then see, two Americans whose values coincided with these attitudinal and ideational tendencies were ready to step up to the proverbial plate just as America decided, in the wake of the Wall Street Panics of 1873, 1893, and especially 1907, that some form of central banking and monetary administration with an elastic currency had become no longer avoidable…

The aforementioned Carter Glass, who hailed from the American South where antifederalist and Jacksonian attitudes long have held sway, was insistent on a design that avoided concentrating financial power in New York or Washington as British central banking had done in London. The also aforementioned Paul Warburg, in turn, was a seasoned German industrial banker who'd immigrated to America, hence a banker well versed in the insistently *productive*, as distinguished from *speculative* modes of banking practiced through commercial paper 'discounting' in highly productive, industrially rapidly growing, non-financialized late nineteenth-century Germany.

Between them, the Chapter concludes, concludes, Glass and Warburg designed a near-perfect Fed for the times, predicated on the aforementioned early twentieth-century rendition of the Real Bills Doctrine (again, 'RBD') to which both founders, like most non-Wall-Street bankers, adhered in the day. The only fly in the proverbial ointment was the one blind spot to which that rendition of the RBD, as noted above, was vulnerable—its assuming sufficiency along with necessity where productive allocation's relation to sound modulation is concerned.

Chapter 3 then tells the tale of the demise of the 1913 Fed and its replacement by the Fed of today. The 1913 understanding of the RBD, this chapter shows, was strong on endogenous money and hence productive allocation, but was weak on exogenous money and hence stable modulation—matters which didn't assume continuously 'existential' import until the modern era with its ever-tighter integration of separate regional and international credit and money markets.[11] This in turn led to the doctrine's unfortunate wholesale 'discrediting' after the financial dramas of the later 1920s.

Blinded as it was to exogenous sources of monetary disturbance as it was thanks to (a) the novelty of now newly transnationally integrating national and international credit markets as well as massive post-WWI German reparations payments, and (b) thralldom to an incomplete, 'Strong Form' of the RBD that all but ignored both rhypothecation risk and the possibility of exogenous money as described in Chapter 2, we find that the Fed failed to act *counter-cyclically*—always a central bank's first duty as far as the modulatory task is concerned. It failed to act counter-cyclically first against the real estate and stock bubbles of the late 1920s fueled both by exogenous money and by rhypothecation, and then against the crash, credit-crunch, and ensuing debt-deflation ('depression') of the early 1930s.[12]

The Fed's failure here, we find, was experienced by both Fed and Congressional policymakers as traumatic and confidence-killing. It thus led ultimately to an over-correction—in this case a frantic abandonment of the RBD altogether, rather than replacing its then 'Strong' formulation with the more refined 'Weak' formulation I give it below. The new view of money and Fed functionality accordingly eschewed attention to endogenous money, production, and productive credit allocation *altogether*, putting all of its chips on the need to counteract exogenous money changes and rehypothecation risk centrally from New York. That effectively meant focusing solely on careful modulation, not productive allocation, of money aggregates—a terrible blunder, we'll see, in effect the symmetrical counterpart of the blunder of the late '20s and early '30s.

This new view found legislative expression in the Banking Act of 1935, which effectively took away the regional Fed District Bank's *raison d'être*—their productive credit-money allocative ('discounting') role—while establishing a new Federal Open Market Committee (again, 'FOMC') dominated by the Federal Reserve Board in DC and the Federal Reserve Bank of New York ('FRBNY,' where the present author used to work) two blocks from Wall Street to focus on modulation alone.

Though this change aided in the task of limiting rehypothecation risk and modulating *exogenous* money aggregates through careful money rental rate control, it could not actually solve the *full* modulation problem without also continuing to attend to the productive (not speculative) *allocation* of *endogenous* money aggregates as the original, pre-1935 Fed had done. That is then what the next Part endeavors to show.

Part II, comprising Chapters 4 through 6, then functions as a theoretical bridge between the early history of Part I's Chapters 1 through 3 and the restorative reform proposals of Part III's Chapters 7 and 8.

Chapter 4 begins by laying out the fundamentals of endogenous credit-money and the combined allocative and modulatory functions that this form of endogeneity presses upon any central bank or monetary authority charged with the task of managing credit-money aggregates. All bank credit denominated as legal tender by a public sector payments system like ours, the Chapter shows, is endogenously generated through lending decisions made by publicly licensed banking institutions. The only limits upon such lending are (a) banks' profit opportunities, determined by those seeking credit, and (b) whatever legal strictures are publicly imposed in the name of liquidity and solvency assurance.

The Chapter then shows how the Fed's founders at least implicitly understood these features of money and the central bank functions that they necessitated. This, the Chapter shows, was reflected in their acceptance of the RBD itself. It also is hardly surprising, as eighteenth- and nineteenth-century observers in both the markets and the academy alike—from John Law through James Steuart and Adam Smith down through Henry Thornton, Karl Marx, Leon Walras and Knut Wicksell—seem uniformly to have held far more nuanced understandings of credit, money, and production than did what later became orthodoxy over the course of the full twentieth century.

Chapter 5 then lays out in detail the RBD as understood in Glass's and Warburg's day, along with what was right and what was wrong about that understanding.[13] It does so, in greater detail, along the general lines adumbrated above—the confounding of necessity with sufficiency characteristic of the old 'Strong-Form RBD,' as I have been calling it, in contrast with the refined 'Weak-Form RBD' that I introduce, formulate, and defend in this Book. The Chapter then shows the Fed's failures of the late 1920s and early 1930s as failures of that earlier, Strong-Form RBD understanding itself.

In this connection, the Chapter also develops my aforementioned revised, modernized and more complete rendition of what the old 1913 vintage RBD unsuccessfully groped for. In essence, this aforementioned

'Refined,' 'Weak-Form' RBD (a) distinguishes carefully between endogenous and exogenous sources of money-generation and money-flow, (b) shows how the functions of money allocation and modulation require different policy approaches to these distinct money forms, and (c) shows how good modulation of money aggregates requires (i) good—again, *productive*—allocation of the endogenous components of those aggregates along with (ii) neutralization (a.k.a. 'sterilization') of exogenously sourced money-flows and (iii) rehypothecation-risk-sensitive rate-setting and OMO in all relevant markets, which include commodity as well as money markets—that is, in *all* markets whose prices are what I've dubbed SIPIS, not just money markets whose prevailing interest rates are but *one species* of that broader genus.

In the course of this exposition, the Chapter also dispatches a number of unfortunate myths and clichés that have hitherto stood in the way of incorporating productive credit allocation back into Fed practice as was done before 1935. Among these are (a) the old saw that officials cannot or ought not to 'pick winners and losers,' (b) the absurd claim that 'productive' investments cannot be distinguished from 'merely speculative' investments, and of course (c) the silly notion, commonly purveyed by and among cranks and ignoramuses, that 'fiat money' is somehow 'inherently' unmanageable and hence inexorably inflationary.

Dogmatic claims of this sort, the Chapter shows, are both theoretically ridiculous (to macro-allocate between productive and speculative investment is not to micro-allocate between business firms), and in any case operationally irrelevant. For it is easy to 'err on the side of liberality' or '-caution' in borderline cases of productive versus speculative investment depending on growth rates and monetary conditions at any given time of policy effectuation and transmission.

That any serious academic, think-tanker, or policymaker repeats such claims can accordingly be attributed only to such people's not having thought through the matter, contenting themselves instead with adherence to what has been unthinking dogma since the ascent to 'conventional wisdom' status of bewildered and bewildering shibboleths from the early 1970s onward. And the best way to do *this* is to restore our cross-regionally distributed, productively allocative, Productive-Republican Fed.

Chapter 6 then takes our story up to the present. It shows how the 1935 reforms proved both well- and ill-advised much as the 1913 design of the Fed had proved well- and ill-advised 'from the other direction.'

In short, we find, the post-1935 inattention to money endogeneity and the associated imperative of productive allocation ultimately doomed the 1935 project of more effective money *modulation itself*. And that, the Chapter makes plain, is for reasons rooted in money endogeneity as laid out and discussed with a view to the imperatives it raises in Chapter 4.

What we missed in 1935 and after was easy to miss for the first several decades following the 1935 reforms, Chapter 6 shows, thanks to the presence of other laws and institutions, put in place during roughly the same New Deal period, that effectively substituted for the pre-1935 allocative Fed. Chief among these were (a) the New Deal and WWII era Reconstruction Finance Corporation ('RFC'), the most massive allocation-attentive special-purpose development bank in history, which actually operated through the Fed's own regionally distributed District Banks; (b) very tight restrictions on interstate banking and branching established or reinforced in the mid-1940s, which kept banking local hence 'Main Street productively' rather than 'Wall Street speculatively' focused; and (c) the Glass-Steagall separation of banking from speculative, as distinguished from productive, investment activity more generally in 1933—yet another instance of Carter Glass's Productive-Republican wisdom in action.

But as the RFC wound-down and disbanded thanks to Cold War paranoia and reactionary 'free-marketeerism' in the 1950s, and as Glass-Steagall separations and bank branching restrictions gave way to similar political and lobbying pressures in the 1980s and 1990s, the consequences of a no-longer allocative Fed grew no longer manageable or concealable—and of course ever more at odds with the American Productive-Republican ideal.

One of these consequences, as Chapter 6 catalogues, is an ever-more hollowed-out productive core of the American economy as Wall Street financial institutions seek profits in speculating and 'outsourcing' American production to cheap-labor jurisdictions. Another is the decline in real wages and hence struggling middle class that have been hallmarks of our nation's past several decades.

This has in turn led to increasing reliance by the American middle class on new forms of consumer, mortgage, 'junk,' and student debt, which in turn have fueled multiple bubbles and busts that bring ever more Fed QE rounds that leave the underlying problem of productive hollowing unaddressed while sowing the seeds for repeated and ever worsening asset and consumer price hyperinflations as the Fed balance sheet and the public debt that afford it the lion's share of its assets expand both indefinitely and still insufficiently productively.

Additional follow-on dysfunctions have of course been worsening wealth and income inequality and social division, followed by political dissensus and breakdown. The only way to 'get our country back,' the Chapter concludes, is to 'get our *Fed* back.' It's to restore our once-great Productive-Republican and industrially diversified economy, localized development banking, and the secure healthy middle class that those things historically enabled.

Part III then turns to the restorative reforms that are the book's ultimate aim—restorations of the smartly distributed, productively allocative and hence successfully modulatory Fed. In so doing, its Chapters show what a 'new, old' Fed predicated on a corrected understanding of the old RBD will look like.

Chapter 7 begins the task of designing a fully updated 1913-style Fed along lines suggested by the historical and theoretical work of the prior chapters. This task is greatly aided, we find, both by the fact that 'we've done this before,' and by the fact that we even began an incipient update like that I design here during the Covid pandemic, in the forms of the Municipal Liquidity Facility ('MLF') and the Main Street Lending ('MSL') programs introduced in 2020.[14]

While flawed in their execution owing to our having vested responsibility for them in only two Federal Reserve District Banks—the New York and Boston Feds—in conception these plans were exceedingly promising, as countless white papers, opinion pieces, and Fed and municipal advisory calls that I put out over 2020–21 made clear. There is no reason, the Chapter accordingly argues, that we can't get those things right now.

The *geographically* '(Re-)Spread Fed' plan that I accordingly blueprint in this Chapter also updates the 1913 distribution of Fed District Banks in a manner that reflects changes our regional economies have undergone over the past century. It makes little sense, for example, to have two Feds in Missouri and only one in California. Happily, this situation is readily rectified without 'taking away' any existing Feds to 'make room' for new ones. We need only make use of the familiar Fed practice of 'branching,' pursuant to which, e.g., the San Francisco Fed maintains a presence in Los Angeles and the Dallas Fed a presence in Houston.

Indeed one of the most providential attributes of the Fed as bequeathed us by Warburg and Glass, I conclude, is its continuing malleability and adaptability. It is truly a central bank that, through sensible and conditions-responsive reform, can endure.

Chapter 8 then turns from *geographical* (re-) distribution to broader *market* (re-) distribution of Fed allocative and modulatory activity. It first reprises my theory of what I have long called 'Systemically Important Prices and Indices'—again, 'SIPIs'—and then shows how a buttressed Fed can modulate non-fundamentals-rooted swings in those markets. In essence, the idea is that certain foodstuff, fuelstuff, and other commodity market prices are subject to massive volatility rooted in what I call Recursive Collective Action Problems and related market failures rather than fundamentals, and these instabilities radiate economy-wide owing to the systemic significance of those prices themselves. Since this is the reason for post-1935 Fed modulatory activity in the money markets themselves via the FOMC and the New York Fed Trading Desk, the Chapter argues, that the Fed must now employ open market operations (again, 'OMO') in these additional markets along with the money markets.

Here too, ironically enough, we shall be partly retrieving Fed origins. For the idea of a 'reserve' implicit in the Fed's origin as a liquidity reserve now is as important an idea to recapture and act upon in other markets whose prices are SIPIs as it is in the money markets the Fed presently acts upon. Fortunately, moreover, the Chicago Fed's new trading floor near the nation's principal commodities exchange—the MERC on Wacker Drive—will enable the Fed to do here what it's long done from its New York trading desk just off Wall Street. The Chapter shows how to do it, carefully designing a mechanism that fully integrates the finance side of commodity OMO, to be conducted by the Chicago Fed, with the 'real' side of the same, to be conducted by our nations strategic stores institutions including the Strategic Petroleum Reserve and the Department of Agriculture's and Department of Defense's counterpart fuelstuff, foodstuff, and strategic metals and rare earths reserves.

The Book's Conclusion reprises the Book's lessons in summary form with a specific five-pillared plan of renewal, while an Appendix following then reduces that plan to specific legislative form in draft bill—a modern counterpart to the 1913 and 1935 legislation discussed in the narrative chapters—to institute the changes designed in the course of Chapters 7 and 8. Happily, I am able to report, a more modest rendition of this very Bill is now before Congress with both House and Senate, bipartisan sponsorship.

Notes

1. Productive-Republicanism, Productivist Central Banking, and their long histories in America will be elaborated in due course throughout this Book. For full book-length and article-length treatments, see Robert Hockett, A Republic of Producers (Yale U. Press 2025); Robert Hockett, *A Jeffersonian Republic by Hamiltonian Means*, 79 So. Cal. L. Rev. 45 (2005); Robert Hockett, *Materializing Citizenship: Finance in a Producers' Republic*, 63 Emory L. Rev. 55 (2013); Robert Hockett, *Pre-Liberal Autonomy and Post-Liberal Finance*, 77 L. & Contemp. Probs. 105 (2014); Robert Hockett, *The Capital Commons: Citizens' Finance in a Productive Commercial Republic*, 39 Journal of Banking & Financial Law 345 (2019–20).
2. The twelve regional Fed district banks, each of which had significant monetary policy autonomy in a sense I'll describe below, were designed to cover regions of the U.S. whose economies were quite different circa 1913. Their specific locations were an entailment of their relative policy autonomy.
3. The term 'discounting,' much more on which below, stems from the particular form that central bank lending took. In essence, the bank purchased short-term debt instruments ('commercial paper') prior to their stated maturities, determining price by discounting the face value of the debt instruments by the prevailing interest rate (since a given face value owed at a later date is worth less at an earlier date). This practice continues to echo in the name of one of the Fed's lending facilities to this day—the 'Discount Window.'
4. By 'monetization,' I mean a central bank's purchase, with spendable legal tender that it itself issues 'from nothing'—vulgarly, 'prints'—of debt or other instruments, such as commercial paper, longer-term promissory notes or bond instruments, that are not themselves legal tender. 'Endogenous money,' in turn, is simply money issued directly or indirectly by central banks in monetizing such instruments as it stands ready on policy grounds to purchase with its own newly issued legal tender in paper, electronic, or digital form. For a brief history of this terrain, see my *Modern, Pre-Modern, or Post-Modern Money? A Brief Guide for the Perplexed*, Forbes, October 26, 2020, at https://www.forbes.com/sites/rhockett/2020/10/26/modern-pre-modern-or-post-modern-money-a-brief-guide-for-the-perplexed/?sh=10b714ec1ae9.
5. Federal Reserve 'Member Banks' are private sector banking institutions that join the Federal Reserve System for access to its liquidity and other facilities. All nationally chartered commercial banks—which are our largest—are required to be Member Banks, while state-chartered banks may either opt-in or opt-out. On the sense in which most American banks

now are 'commercial' banks, see Part I below. In brief, these banks originally emerged to finance productive firms by accepting and discounting short-term debt instruments—'commercial paper'—issued by those firms, which paper was monetizable by the Federal Reserve's regional District Banks in the sense defined in notes 3 and 4 above.

6. I say 'not merely profits' because non-productive speculative investments—e.g., mere gambling—can be profitable too. I might make a killing in Vegas, for example, in which case I have produced nothing but simply transferred preexisting wealth fro the casino to myself. When critics compare Wall Street at this point—alas, not altogether unfairly—to 'a casino,' or refer to 'casino capitalism,' this is what they're alluding to; a financial system that transfers wealth rather than productively assisting in the *production or generation* of wealth. See, e.g., my *Building Banks Better: A Plan to Put Public Capital Back to Public Use*, 5 Stanford Journal of Blockchain Law & Policy 1 (2022), at https://papers.ssrn.com/sol3/papers.cfm?abstract_id=4023614.
7. I introduced attention to the importance of distinguishing the allocation and modulation functions associated with these terms in the wake of the Crash of 2008. See Robert Hockett, *A Fixer-Upper for Finance*, 87 Washington University Law Review 1 (2009), at https://papers.ssrn.com/sol3/papers.cfm?abstract_id=1367278. For a concise description of these functions in connection with a renewed 'discounting' Fed, see again my recently contributed book chapter, Robert Hockett, *Scissors Require Two Blades*, in Populism and the Future of the Fed (James A. Dorn ed. 2022), at https://papers.ssrn.com/sol3/papers.cfm?abstract_id=3918988. The book describes the theory and the intellectual milieu in which the RBD was at home at substantial, but I hope not tedious, length.

   There are many fine histories on the subject from which I draw freely. See, e.g., J. Laurence Laughlin, The Principles of Money (Scribners 1903); E.A. Goldenweiser, The Federal Reserve System in Operation (McGraw-Hill 1925); W.R. Burgess, The Reserve Banks and the Money Market (Harper, 1927); Lloyd W. Mints, A History of Banking Theory in Great Britain and the United States (U. Chi. Press 1945); E.A. Goldenweiser, American Monetary Policy (McGraw-Hill 1951); Lester V. Chandler, Benjamin Strong, Central Banker (Brookings 1958); Milton Friedman & Anna Schwartz, A Monetary History of the United States, 1867–1960 (Princeton U. Press 1963); Elmus Wicker, Federal Reserve Monetary Policy, 1917–1933 (Random House 1966); Robert Craig West, Banking Reform and the Federal Reserve: 1863–1923 (Cornell U. Press 1974); Bray Hammond, Banks and Politics in America from the Revolution to the Civil War (Princeton U. Press 1991); Alan Meltzer, A History of the Federal Reserve, Volumes 1 and 2 (Brookings 2004–2010); Richard

H. Timberlake, Monetary Policy in the United States: An Intellectual and Institutional History (U. Chi. Press 1993); and Thomas M. Humphrey & Richard H. Timberlake, Gold, the Real Bills Doctrine, and the Fed: Sources of Monetary Disorder, 1922–1938 (Cato 2019). Because most these sources are all old by now, I hope that my book will also serve as a helpful contemporary addition to this literature. For a summary account, see my recent book chapter, Robert Hockett, *Scissors Require Two Blades*, in Populism and the Future of the Fed (Cato, James A. Dorn ed. 2022), at https://papers.ssrn.com/sol3/papers.cfm?abstract_id=3918988.

8. See again note 3, above, and its associated text 'above the line.'
9. See again note 5, above, and its associated text 'above the line.'
10. And of course *both* (a) and (b) can be true at various times. So while the 1913 rendition of the RBD was right in holding that the Fed's productive allocation of credit-money was *necessary* to sound modulation, it was wrong in suggesting that it was *sufficient* to that end as well.
11. Please see again notes 3 and 5, above, if these terms still ring unfamiliar. I introduced attention to the importance of distinguishing the allocation and modulation functions associated with these terms in the wake of the Crash of 2008. See Robert Hockett, *A Fixer-Upper for Finance*, 87 Washington University Law Review 1 (2009), at https://papers.ssrn.com/sol3/papers.cfm?abstract_id=1367278. For a concise description of these functions in connection with a renewed 'discounting' Fed, see again my recently contributed book chapter, Robert Hockett, *Scissors Require Two Blades*, in Populism and the Future of the Fed (James A. Dorn ed. 2022), at https://papers.ssrn.com/sol3/papers.cfm?abstract_id=3918988.
12. Again, the gold standard exacerbated the error. Incidentally, I refer to such action as 'counter-cyclical' pursuant to my long-advocated view of central banks' primary role, vis-à-vis fluctuations in money aggregates not rooted in 'fundamentals,' understood as real goods and services supplies that 'absorb' money. I characterize this role as that of a massive public-sector 'market-mover' or market 'contrarian.' See, e.g., Robert Hockett, *Recursive Collective Action Problems: The Structure of Procyclicality in Money Markets, Macroeconomies, and Formally Similar Contexts*, 3 Journal of Financial Perspectives 1 (2013), at https://papers.ssrn.com/sol3/papers.cfm?abstract_id=2239849. There will be more on this, of course, below, especially in Part II.
13. Please see the footnotes above. A brief history of this terrain, again, is my *Modern, Pre-Modern, or Post-Modern Money? A Brief Guide for the Perplexed*, Forbes, October 26, 2020, at https://www.forbes.com/sites/rhockett/2020/10/26/modern-pre-modern-or-post-modern-money-a-brief-guide-for-the-perplexed/?sh=10b714ec1ae9.

14. See my Forbes page and my SSRN page for a plethora of columns and white papers I put out on how to optimize these programs over 2020 and 2021.

Contents

About the Author

Robert C. Hockett has published multiple books and articles at the intersection of law, finance, and philosophy. He is the Edward Cornell Professor of Law and Finance at Cornell University, where he teaches Enterprise-Organizational, Finance-Regulatory, and Public Finance law as well as Central Banking, Monetary Theory, and other, more philosophical subjects. He is also a regular Visiting Professor of Finance at Georgetown University McDonough School of Business; and is Senior Counsel at Westwood Capital, LLC, a socially conscious investment bank in Midtown Manhattan.

Hockett serves on the Advisory Board of the Public Banking Institute; the Advisory Board of the Stanford Digital Currency Lab; the BerkShares Community Currency Project in rural Massachusetts; and, as a Founding Member, on the Board of the Digital Fiat Currency Institute headquartered in Hong Kong. He is a regular advisor and legislative draftsman for Senators Bernie Sanders, Elizabeth Warren, Marco Rubio, and others in the US Senate, as well as for Representatives Alexandria Ocasio-Cortez, Ro Khanna, and others in the US House of Representatives.

Hockett is perhaps best known for (a) having co-conceived and co-drafted Rep. Ocasio-Cortez's Green New Deal Resolution and Finance Plan; (b) the 'Eminent Domain' Plan for underwater mortgage loans adopted by many foreclosure-struck municipalities during the last financial crisis; and (c) numerous pieces of recent legislation for Rep. Khanna and Sen. Rubio both jointly and severally. Formerly with the Federal

Reserve Bank of New York and the International Monetary Fund, Hockett has published many books and articles in his fields of expertise. A Rhodes Scholar, he earned his undergraduate and advanced degrees at Kansas, Oxford, and Yale Universities.

List of Figures

PART I

Loving and Hating On Collective Political Agency–Three Productive-Republican Monetary Histories

The fact is well known among constitutional lawyers and historians: the American republic has long been of two minds where centralizing governance among distinct political units with actual or vicarious histories of mutual independence is concerned.[1] Both minds are broadly what I have elsewhere called 'Productive-Republican'—that is, rooted in a vision of broadly autonomous, prosperous producer-citizens. But they have differed over what mode of polity best enables the Productive-Republican vision's realization.

Our first experiment with a written national constitution, the Articles of Confederation, was notoriously stingy in its grant of authority, powers, and functionality to the 'central' government, which some (far from all) founders feared would inevitably grow powerful enough to threaten Productive-Republican liberty. Indeed it was so stingy on this score that the arrangement quickly came as a cropper as 'the several states' succumbed to a multitude of collective action problems that they had no adequate mode of collective agency to address.

Those problems struck mainly at interstate commerce hence economic integration, which is why (a) the move to replace the Articles began as an interstate convention on 'trade and navigation,' and (b) the most potent addition to the new constitution turned out to be its Commerce Clause.

[1] 'Vicarious' because states the entered our union after 1788 were, with the exceptions of California and Texas, never independent political units, but instead thought of themselves as akin to the original thirteen states that, in an attenuated sense, had been.

Hence, while we began, constitutionally speaking, as full Jeffersonians, we soon learned we would have to be Hamiltonians or Madisonians too.[2]

The Constitution that replaced the Articles at the end of the 1780s, in which Mr. Hamilton himself had the most significant hand, looked much more promising on paper than had its predecessor.[3] Its Commerce Clause in particular, giving the newly empowered national legislature—Congress—overriding jurisdiction over all matters affecting the full integration and smooth functioning of a truly national economy, would prove in short order to be one of its principal achievements. But as Hamilton, Madison, and other advocates learned, its ratification was not easy. And 'facts on the ground,' where citizen attitudes were concerned, did not universally synch well with the new document's content until many national controversies, and at least one civil war, later.[4]

Indeed even today the historic ambivalence remains. It even and once again threatens our national unity as political parties grow ever more regional in character and states once again speak of secession—first jokingly, then something resembling more seriously.[5] Our Jeffersonian-Hamiltonian polarity and associated 'dialectical' oscillation—our national 'mark of Cain,' as it were—continues to mark who 'we' are.[6]

While the broad outlines of our cycling federalist-antifederalist dialectic are reasonably well known among lawyers and historians, the ways that

[2] See again Robert Hockett, A Republic of Producers (Yale U. Press 2025). See also Robert Hockett, A Jeffersonian Republic by Hamiltonian Means, 79 So. Cal. L. Rev. 45 (2005); Robert Hockett, Materializing Citizenship: Finance in a Producers' Republic, 63 Emory L. Rev. 55 (2013); Robert Hockett, Pre-Liberal Autonomy and Post-Liberal Finance, 77 L. & Contemp. Probs. 105 (2014); Robert Hockett, The Capital Commons: Citizens' Finance in a Productive Commercial Republic, 39 Journal of Banking & Financial Law 345 (2019-20).

[3] Hamilton had a hand not only in drafting the new constitution in the name of replacing what he called 'imbecile' executive capacity with effective executive capacity, but also in ensuring ratification (he wrote nearly ¾ of 'The Federalist') and, as importantly, organizing the call or a new constitutional convention itself. It would be difficult to overestimate all that our federal republic and combined fiscal and monetary systems owe this one fellow. See Hockett, sources cited id.

[4] Hockett, Capital Commons, supra note 16.

[5] See, e.g., Chuck Thompson, Better Off Without 'Em: A Northern Manifesto for Southern Secession (2012).

[6] See sources cited supra, note 16.

our money and public finance have traveled this path remain less so.[7] But travel that pathway they do, from the (a) 'now you see it, now you don't' flickering of early central banking and currency issuance on the part of Hamilton's First and Gallatin's Second Banks of the U.S. in the late eighteenth and early nineteenth centuries, through (b) the banking and currency reforms of the mid-1860s which brought us our still-present 'Greenback' dollar bills and our system of 'national banks,' on down to (c) the long evolution of the Federal Reserve System, the Treasury with which it routinely collaborates, and banking thereunder from 1913 to the present.[8]

Let us begin, with that pre-Fed history, then turn to early Fed history itself and what followed...

[7] Id.

[8] Id. See also Robert Hockett, Money's Past is Fintech's Future: Wildcat Crypto, the Digital Dollar, and Citizens Central Banking, 2 Stanford J. Blockchain L. & Pol'y 1 (2019).

CHAPTER 1

Three Ages and Stages of American Money

Abstract This Chapter sets the stage of Part I and the rest of the Book by recounting America's troubled history with money and central banking from the Founding Era to 1913. In particular, it shows how our historical oscillations between favoring centralized banking and disfavoring it parallel the American polity's broader oscillations between favoring federal and public sector capacity on the one hand, state and private sector prerogatives on the other. It is no accident, we find, that Alexander Hamilton's First Bank of the U.S., which functioned as a combined money-allocating central and industry-promoting national development bank, coincided with the ascendancy of the Federalists and the new centralizing Constitution they promulgated. Nor is it an accident that our first experiment with such banking ended with the ascendancy to the White House of our most militantly *anti*-Federalist President, Andrew Jackson. It is also no accident, this Chapter indicates, that the first *still-enduring* establishment of federal supremacy over matters monetary comes with the *Civil War*, which both settled the question of federal supremacy in our constitutional order once and for all, *and* bequeathed us the national banking system, the national bank chartering authority and activity regulator (the Office of the Comptroller of the Currency ('OCC') still within Treasury), and the currency (the 'greenback' dollar bill) that we use to this day even after transfer of issuance from Treasury to the Fed. Our monetary and central banking dialectic, the Chapter concludes,

R. C. Hockett, *Spread the Fed*,
https://doi.org/10.1007/978-3-031-72051-2_1

just is our federal versus state and our public versus private dialectics as refracted in the realm of finance.

Keywords Anti-Federalists · Banking · Central Banking · Civil War · Dollar · Federalism · Federalists · Federal Reserve System · 'Free' Banking · Greenbacks · Hamilton · Jackson · OCC · Productivism · Productivist Central Banking · Productive-Republicanism · Republicanism · 'Wildcat Banking.'

Dollar bills are remarkable things. They're the same all over the U.S.. Take out money from a bank branch or an ATM anywhere and you'll get the same thing for your trouble: a combination of green one dollar, five dollar, ten dollar, twenty dollar or perhaps hundred dollar notes. They'll all look the same, and they all will be worth the same when their denominations are the same.

That is what sovereign-issued currency looks like, even when paid out or lent out by nominally 'private' banks. Because they all deal in national currencies, banks are not really as private as you might think. They are licensed by us, the sovereign public, to deal in our money—our Federal Reserve Notes, as our money bills call themselves.[1]

'Dealing in' our money here includes several things, among them taking deposits in the form of that money, administering payments made via resultant *accounts* that hold deposited money, and even *issuing* our money, every time they make loans, which they do simply by crediting or opening dollar-denominated accounts directly. The latter is a process that, contrary to popular misconception, requires no antecedent accumulation of deposited funds. All that is needed is for the Fed to recognize payments made from these bank-opened or -credited accounts via the national payments system that it administers, a process that I call 'accommodation.'

In effect, then, banks are franchisees, while we the sovereign public are the franchisor and our national money—the dollar, the monetized full faith and credit of the U.S.—is the franchised good.[2]

You can think of the uniform value and appearance of our currency as being a bit like those identical sandwiches and golden arches you see all around the country (and world) if you like: They serve to let everyone know that the item's the same irrespective of just where you are in our nation—New York, California; Florida, Alaska … They are always and everywhere the same: green notes, worth no more and no less that they purport to be worth.

And if a bank abuses the brand by, say, issuing bad loans or over-levering itself, thereby imperiling the value of deposits, it will risk losing its charter much as a restaurateur who sells spoiled food risks being booted from the franchise. That's how franchises work. They are 'quality control' pacts, with the franchisees abiding by the terms and the franchisor administering and enforcing the terms. Where our money's concerned, we are the franchisor.[3]

If you see the truth in this, you might be tempted to think things have always been thus. Didn't the U.S. make the dollar its money right from the start? Isn't it in the Constitution or something?

The answer is, 'yes and no.' The key feature of the dollar in the early days of our republic—until 1863—is that for most of these years it was primarily a mere unit of account rather than a currency. Sure, the U.S. Mint minted coins, the Treasury issued some paper and the First and Second Banks of the U.S. issued some paper as well from the 1790s to 1836. But paper money—'notes'—were issued primarily by private banking institutions, whose strong or weak regulation was denied the federal government by anti-federalist Jacksonians in favor of the states, until late in the nineteenth century. Hence the term 'bank notes' for most paper currencies that circulated until late in the nineteenth century. America's paper money supply was primarily a plethora of privately issued, at most state-regulated 'bank notes.'[4]

Bank notes were denominated in dollar increments, but were not sovereign-issued liabilities like today's dollar bills are. To recur to my earlier metaphor, the banks were at best franchisees of subnational state governments alike, and at worst franchisees of themselves. Their notes were their own liabilities—hence liabilities of private issuers. And different issuers, for their part, were differently reliable. Two banks might both promise redeemability of their notes into the same quantum of something more solid—gold, for example, or U.S. Treasury certificates—but might well be differently able to live up to their promises. Some might be sound, others might be less so. Some might be sound this year but not so much next year.

These differences among banks' reliability stemmed from a variety of factors. One was that bank regulation was more technologically difficult in the nineteenth century, meaning that regulators could be only so effective at enforcing licensure requirements and exercising 'quality control' over paper currency issuers. Another was that banks then were chartered and regulated, as noted above, Antifederalist fashion by states rather than by our federal government. This meant that differing state willingness or readiness to regulate could bring differing values to currencies issued in different locales. New York and New England banks, for example, were often reliable. Nebraska or Michigan banks, by contrast, not so much.

The upshot of this 'Banking Babel'[5] was that the nation's currency supply largely consisted of hundreds or thousands of distinct bank notes all trading at various discounts to stated par. A dollar note issued by Billy the Kid Bank or Sidewinder Bank might trade at 50% of par, for example, amounting to no more than 'four bits,' not a dollar. A dollar note issued by Wyatt Erp Bank or Bald Eagle Bank might, by contrast, go for 90% of par, or even full par.

Making things worse, these currencies constantly *fluctuated* in value, both in relation to the goods and services they could command and in relation to *one another*. 'How much money' you had in your pocket thus varied with whose notes you carried and when, even though all were denominated in dollars. Shopkeepers and tradesmen in consequence had to maintain regularly updated discount schedules behind their counters, instructing clerks how much to discount different banks' notes in determining 'how much' (of what) to charge buyers for goods or for services.

If you carried multiple banks' notes in your pockets, making purchases at the general store could take you—and the store clerk—much longer than we're used to by now. Imagine the queues that would form at the 'checkout lines' of our stores if we did that now... Scarce wonder that this period of U.S. banking history is called the 'wildcat banking' era.[6] (Those who think this was a good idea call it the 'free banking' era. It was free all right—often value-free.)

Needless to say, private banknote money did not make for an optimal payment system. It was good that the nation had a *unit of account*—the dollar—but unfortunately it still lacked a widely usable national *currency*.

This all began to change in the early 1860s. By that time the nation was embroiled in domestic strife. The Civil War, which was simply the most dramatic (and destructive) manifestation to date of the Federalist/Antifederalist dialectic noted above, threw up two factors that made something resembling a uniform national currency possible.

The first factor was that the stresses of war made a single and stable currency more clearly necessary than ever before. To prosecute the war the federal government had to be able to spend its own currency anywhere in the union where government operations were necessary. The second factor was that the southern slave states, which had always been the principal Antifederalist objectors to federal banking and national monetary uniformity, were conveniently unrepresented in Congress during the war years—they were the states trying to secede.

The upshot was that Congress passed a number of pieces of currency reform legislation, culminating in the Legal Tender Act of 1862, the National Currency Act of 1863, and the National Banking Act of 1864,[7] all signed into law by President Lincoln. The Acts together established a system of federally chartered 'National Banks,' located all over the nation, all issuing notes convertible into the very same Treasury-issued currency. The latter was called, tellingly, the 'Greenback.' That color word linked to a currency might ring familiar.

The banking and currency acts of the 1860s transformed our interlinked banking, financial, and monetary systems. In very short order there were federally chartered banks in most states and territories of the Union, all of them subject to uniform regulatory standards—including that every $100 in notes be backed by $111 in sovereign bonds—and all of them issuing, accordingly, a de facto uniform currency with a uniform value. These banks could also sell U.S. Treasury securities, effectively making them a system of outlets for issuance of *both* of our federal government's principal circulating liabilities—Greenback *dollar* bills and, as it were, *T*-Bills. In very little time, inferior privately issued 'wildcat' banknotes drained out of circulation.

The administrator of the new national banking system was called, tellingly, the Office of the Comptroller of the Currency, or 'OCC,' housed in the Treasury Department.[8] The name is telling because 'comptroller' is merely archaic English for 'controller.' The OCC, again, significantly housed within the National Treasury, was effectively the 'controller'—the administrator—of our national currency system. That, and only that, was why the OCC was founded as the nation's first federal bank regulator. It is almost as if Congress and President Lincoln understood, at least implicitly, that they were establishing a sort of national sovereign money franchise, not just a 'bank regulator.'[9]

The OCC remains to this day one of the U.S.' three principal federal bank regulators. It is the chartering authority for national banks, administers those banks' portfolio-regulatory and other regulatory regimes, and has final word on whether a national bank has gone bankrupt in such manner as engages the orderly liquidation and depositor reimbursement processes prescribed by the Federal Deposit Insurance Act promulgated some 70 years after the 1860s banking and currency enactments—during the Great Depression and responsive New Deal of the 1930s, as discussed more fully below.

The OCC now has rather less to do with the national currency, however, than it had for its first fifty years. That is because, by 1913, we as a nation had come to realize that a healthy economy needed more than a *uniform* currency. It *also* needed what is known in the discipline as an *elastic* currency.[10] Or, to put the matter only a little differently with an eye on uniformity as such, it needed a currency that is both geographically *and inter-temporally* uniform—stable, not inflating or deflating, reliable in terms of the goods and services it could command over time.

An elastic currency is a currency whose supply can be adjusted (a) to accommodate, while not *over*-accommodating, transaction and credit, hence also productive investment demand, and (b) to counteract sudden credit or other, more exogenously sourced, supply expansions or contractions.[11] The idea is to maintain just enough credit-money supply to accommodate desired transaction volumes and enable productive investment so as not needlessly to squelch or forgo either, while at the same time preventing over-issuance of the sort that can spark inflation—the classic problem of 'too much money' chasing 'too few goods.'[12]

A money whose supply can be 'modulated' in this way, as I call it, is essential if we're to avoid needlessly disrupting either transaction activity, investment activity, or currency value.[13] And that is to say it's essential if we would maintain smooth, steady growth of our nation's wealth and productive capacity.

The OCC and Treasury more generally were not well equipped, operationally or transaction-technologically speaking, to engage in what I elsewhere call this daily 'money-modulatory' task that an elastic currency requires—at least not so long as state-chartered banks offering checkable deposits continued to operate alongside the national banking system. The Second Bank of the U.S. from 1816 to 1836, and especially central banks of the kind found all over the 'developed' world circa 1913, by contrast, had shown themselves well suited to the task. By acting as 'banks to the banks,' these institutions were able to modulate private bank money-issuance in ever more 'fine-tuned' manners, using 'carrots' as effectively as 'sticks.'

The U.S. accordingly established its version of a central bank, patterned partly on European models and partly on privately ordered clearinghouse arrangements among private sector banks that had emerged in New York and New England, with the Federal Reserve Act of 1913.[14] Like the banking acts of the 1860s, this change too was proximately occasioned by crisis—in this case, the panics of 1873, 1893, and especially 1907.

The Federal Reserve Act ('FRA') of 1913, as we'll shortly see in more detail, established the Fed that we all know today, and transferred de facto *and* de jure administration of the national money supply primarily from the Comptroller to this new entity. This is why the 'Greenbacks' you now find in your pocket call themselves, not 'Treasury Notes,' but 'Federal Reserve Notes.' So we now again use 'bank notes' as currency just as we did in the nineteenth century. It's just that they're *public* bank notes—'central' bank notes—rather than *private* bank notes now. They are *Citizen* Notes, you might say. They are issued and spent in the name of us all—the citizenry of our Productive Republic.

And what is true of Federal Reserve Notes here is true of bank credit extended in Fed Note—that is, dollar—increments too. The loan the bank makes to you in the form of a newly opened or credited deposit it 'makes' in the form of dollar-denominated withdrawal or spending rights. The deposits, in other words, are functional equivalents of dollar bills. That is why Wicksell dubbed bank credit 'bank money,' and why both Marx before him and then Keynes and others after him have called it 'credit-money.'

Once you realize this, and once you remind yourself both that those dollars are Fed 'Notes' and that you give the bank a signed *promissory* note for your *loan*, you are able to see something else too: This is that a loan is simply a *temporary swap* of *your* promissory note for *Fed* promissory notes—of your privately issued money for more widely spendable publicly issued money. Bank lending is just temporary private–public currency swapping. That will prove important when we shift focus to the importance of money endogeneity below.

This is yet another sense, incidentally, in which banks are franchisees of our money, with 'we, the people'—the citizenry of our Productive Republic—occupying the role of franchisor. In effect, we 'outsource' the credit-checking and public money-dispensary function to private sector franchisee institutions. We do so on the theory that they're 'closer to the ground' than our central bank is when it comes to determining what private–public promissory note swaps, which convey purchasing power in trust to those lacking it, are apt to be put to good—that is, productive—use. And we let them charge 'interest'—a sort of 'privatized seignorage,' as I call it—for their trouble.[15]

This is, with the modifications to be laid out below, the money system we now have—the public–private franchise system that issues our endogenous credit-money. It allowed for a currency that was what I call spatially uniform—across the entire republic—but not what I call temporally uniform. That takes us on to the establishment of the Fed.

Notes

1. See Robert Hockett, *Finance without Financiers*, in Real Utopias: Democratizing Finance (Fred Block & Robert Hockett, eds., 2022); Robert Hockett, *Finance without Financiers*, 47 Politics & Society 1 (2019); *Rousseauvian Money*, working paper (2018), available at https://papers.ssrn.com/sol3/papers.cfm?abstract_id=3278408.
2. Id. Also Robert C. Hockett, *The Finance Franchise*, 102 Cornell L. R. 1143 (2017).
3. See sources cited id. Also Robert Hockett, *The Citizens' Ledger: Digitizing Our Money, Democratizing Our Finance* (Palgrave, 2022).
4. See Hockett, *Citizens' Ledger*, id.; and Hockett, *Rousseauvian Money*, supra note 1.
5. See Robert Hockett, *Cryptocurrencies Explained*, TYT Interviews with Cenk Uygur and Nomiki Konst, February 2018, available at https://www.youtube.com/watch?v=qdR4ujneQzo.
6. Id. Also Hockett, sources cited supra, notes 1, 2, and 3.
7. Legal Tender Act of 1862, ch. 142, 12 Stat. 532; July 11, 1862. National Currency Act of 1863, ch. 58, 12 Stat. 665; February 25, 1863. National Banking Act of 1864, ch. 106, 13 Stat. 99; June 3, 1864.
8. Id. See also OCC homepage, available at https://www.occ.treas.gov/.
9. See again Hockett, sources cited supra, notes 1, 2, and 3.
10. Id.

11. Id.
12. Id.
13. Id. Also Robert Hockett, *A Fixer-Upper for Finance*, 87 Wash. U. L. Rev. 1213 (2010).
14. Federal Reserve Act, ch. 6, 38 Stat. 251; December 23, 1913. See generally https://www.federalreserve.gov/aboutthefed/fract.htm.
15. For more on seignorage and its privatization, see Hockett, sources cited supra, notes 1, 2, 3, and 5.

CHAPTER 2

Central Banking with Federalist Characteristics: The Coming of the Productive-Republican Fed

Abstract This Chapter turns to the Fed's founding era and, for heuristic purposes, in only broadbrush form, its early 'operating system'—the Real Bills Doctrine The emphasis is on how we at last came to find central banking unavoidable in a modern, industrial economy on the one hand, while having to satisfy that need via what I call 'central banking with federalist characteristics' on the other hand. The characteristics I emphasize are a *'distributed,' federated structure*—'decentralization'—on the one hand, and a favoring of 'Main Street' *production* over 'Wall Street' *speculation* on the other. Happily, two Americans whose values coincided with these attitudinal and ideational tendencies were ready to step up to the proverbial plate just as America decided, in the wake of the Wall Street Panics of 1873, 1893, and especially 1907, that some form of central banking had become no longer avoidable. Carter Glass and Paul Warburg. Glass, who hailed from the American South where Jacksonian Antifederalist attitudes long had held sway, was insistent on a design that avoided concentrating financial power in New York or Washington as British central banking had done in London. Warburg, in turn, was a seasoned German industrial banker who had immigrated to America, hence a banker well versed in the exclusively *productive*, as distinguished from *speculative* modes of banking practiced through commercial paper 'discounting' in highly productive, industrially rapidly growing, non-financialized late nineteenth century Germany. Between

R. C. Hockett, *Spread the Fed*,
https://doi.org/10.1007/978-3-031-72051-2_2

them, Glass and Warburg designed a near-perfect Fed, predicated on an early twentieth-century rendition of the highly Productivist Real Bills Doctrine ('RBD'). The only fly in the proverbial ointment was the one blind-spot to which that rendition of the RBD, as discussed more fully in this Book's subsequent Chapters, was vulnerable.

Keywords Anti-Federalists · Banking · Central Banking · Discounting · Dollar · Elastic Currency · Fed District Banks · Federalism · Federalists · Federal Reserve Board · Federal Reserve System · 'Free' Banking · German Banking · Greenbacks · Glass · Industrialization · Panics · Productivism · Productivist Central Banking · Productive-Republicanism · Real Bills Doctrine · Republicanism · Speculation · Warburg

Centralized *issuance* of a currency in the name of spatial or geographical uniformity—uniformity across the nation's multiple regions, as came in the 1860s—is one thing. Centralized *modulation* of currency supplies in the cause of *temporal* uniformity—that is, continuous money supply management in relation to goods and services aggregates in the name of avoiding inflation and deflation—is quite another.[1] The need of latter, the U.S. at last learned at the turn of the nineteenth and twentieth centuries, is the need of what both Hamilton in the U.S. and his counterparts abroad had long known as the need of a central bank or other modulatorily-enabled monetary authority.

Thanks to the U.S.' longstanding ambivalence about central government, banking, and central banking as noted above and further elaborated upon below, however, the Federal Reserve System as first designed and then instituted embodied a delicate compromise. On the one hand, the Federal Reserve Board at the apex of the Federal Reserve System would operate nationwide as a liquidity risk-pooling authority and national policy-coordinator and money-modulator. Those are two functions that any 'central' bank worth the name has to discharge.[2]

On the other hand, the Federal Reserve '*System*,' unlike the Holy Roman Empire as described by Voltaire, would indeed be both *federated* and a '*system*,' a system that *also* would manifest public–private *hybridity*.[3] This, it seems to have been thought at the time, would remove the two principal 'holdups' that had traditionally stood in the way of successfully instituting and retaining an American central bank. Those were the fears (a) of financial and hence productive dominance by northeastern money center banks, and (b) of a putatively oversized or even 'socialist' public sector.[4]

The principal means by which the Federal Reserve System addressed and allayed these concerns was through what I call its 'distributed' system of *regional* Federal Reserve '*District Banks*,' in the plural. These would serve as the full System's primary 'interface' with private sector commercial (I do not say 'financial') and manufacturing activity nationwide. The regional Feds, as I'll sometimes call them, were assigned specific territorial jurisdictions, in a manner roughly tracking the 'Circuit' system of federal appellate courts with which all who engage with American law become quickly familiar.[5]

The background understanding against which the Fed's federated structure was designed was that the national economy circa 1913 roughly divided into distinct, not-yet-fully-integrated regions in which particular industries and particular cultures of credit and financial practice held particular importance.[6] Most of these regions were of course east of the Rocky Mountains at that time, which is why to this day we find two Feds in Missouri, eight east of there, and only two west of the Rockies.[7]

In New York and Boston, for example, finance and manufacturing were predominant, as were the large investment 'houses' that often organized groups of small firms into more sprawling industrial and infrastructural conglomerates—notably railroads, petroleum, and in time (a bit further west), autos and steel.[8] In the Midwest it was first mainly agriculture, dairy, meat processing, small-scale agricultural finance, and community banking that prevailed. In the Southwest both ranching and petroleum were growth sectors with idiosyncratic modes of financing, while in the Southeast it was primarily cash crops, coal, and personal lending or highly localized banking that prevailed.[9]

The thought that the Federal Reserve Act's (FRA's) framers appear to have entertained, then, was that each intelligibly distinct region of the country where finance and production were concerned had access to its own Fed discount and lending facilities, along with a means by which to communicate on a regular basis with the nationwide Fed 'System.'[10] This, they believed, would avert the danger of a European style of central banking too wedded to any one region, sector, or set of financial interests or practices.[11]

A collateral thought seems to have been harbored by 'nationalist' Progressives in the mold of Theodor Roosevelt, Walter Lipmann, and Herbert Croly. It was that by 'distributing,' as I call it, Fed operations regionally, we would also put into place a potent institutional mechanism that might facilitate inter-regional convergence on certain would-be universal 'best practices.' That in turn could complete the process of full nationwide economic integration and ascent to 'great power' status that had already proved long in coming.[12]

As it happened, the regionalist answer to the set of 'regionalist' concerns just elaborated also afforded means of addressing the *other* set of concerns. I mean the set rooted in fears of 'government overreach' and 'socialism' in a time of labor militancy, heightened immigration from southern and eastern European hotbeds of 'Anarchism,' and a now rapidly developing 'administrative state.'[13]

Key here was the regional Feds' ownership and associated governance structures. In essence, the regional Fed Banks would be owned—in a novel and rather thin sense of 'owning'—by their private sector Member Banks, even while overseen from the Fed Board in Washington.[14] In addition, each Fed Bank would be overseen by a 9-member board three of whose members would be chosen by the Fed Board in DC, three others of whom would be selected by local Member Banks, and the remaining three of whom would be chosen by non-financial local businesses and labor organizations.[15]

This would, it appears to have been thought, render the Fed System something more like a public–private partnership than a 'command and control' style federal regulator of the sort that was already proliferating by 1913. It also would further enshrine those forms of regional and sectoral pluralism that anti-centralizers had been keen to preserve through the nation's history to that point.[16] It would be a Fed that, like the nation itself, was simultaneously Hamiltonian and Jeffersonian.[17]

Additionally crucial to the first Fed, as we shall see in much greater detail presently, was its focus on production as distinguished from speculation. The Fed's founders were acutely aware of the distinction between non-inflationary and wealth-generating productive investment on the one hand, and merely bubble-inflating and wealth-redistributing financial speculation on the other hand. This understanding lay at the core of the Real Bills Doctrine (again, 'RBD') that constituted the early Fed's operating system as we'll see below. It also, accordingly, determined the eligibility criteria that all the Regional Feds employed in its lending, not to mention its adoption of the World War I era War Industries Board's Index of Production in evaluating the successes or otherwise of its lending.

The upshot of this 1913 settlement was that in its earliest decades the Fed as a 'System' was nontrivially 'diffuse' and 'distributed' in a way mirroring the still-incomplete integration of national governance and the national economy themselves.[18] Regional economic and cultural differences could accordingly play discernible, even if not fully dispositive, roles in determining Fed policy across regions.[19] In addition, all regions were made more hospitable to productive industries that could flourish in their environments, rather than to mere hucksters and speculators who redistributed wealth rather than generating it.

As years passed and the nation's economy and political cultures grew more integrated and less heterogeneous at an accelerating rate, however, the Fed itself grew more practically unitary in tandem.[20] And increasingly worrisome episodes of financial volatility, themselves rooted partly in that integration, raised the stakes involved in the process.[21] These developments, we shall see, all stemmed from one subtle error in the Fed's operating system—its mistaking productive credit allocation's *necessity* to macroeconomic stability for its *sufficiency* to the same.

NOTES

1. We'll have much more to say about what I call modulation and its complement, allocation, below. For reminder of the distinction, which I introduced in 2008, see again Hockett, Fixer-Upper, supra Chapter Frontmatter, note 11.
2. In taking on the liquidity risk pooling function, the Fed simply took over, in the interest of fuller and hence more effective pooling, the system of ad hoc 'clearinghouse' arrangements that private sector banking institutions had developed in the preceding decades. I call this oft-repeated form of finance-regulatory upgrade 'The Commandeering Model,' of which there are many other examples. See Robert Hockett, *The (Regulatory) Dialectic of Finance* (working paper, 2017). As for money modulation, its necessity, and central banks' centrality to its effectuation, see Hockett, *Capital Commons*, supra Part I, note 2. See also Robert Hockett, *A Fixer-Upper for Finance*, 97 Wash. U. L. Rev. 1213 (2009) (introducing and christening the idea); Robert Hockett, *Bretton Woods 1.0: An Essay in Constructive Retrieval*, 16 N.Y.U. J. L. & Pol'y

401 (2010) (explaining why successful domestic discharge of the modulatory task requires an accommodative non-national global central bank, and designing one); Robert Hockett, *Finance without Financiers*, in Democratizing Finance [2015], supra Chapter 1, note 1; Robert Hockett, *Rousseauvian Money* (working paper 2018).

3. I allude to Voltaire's oft-quoted quip that the Holy Roman Empire was neither holy, Roman, nor an empire.
4. See again Hockett, *Capital Commons*, supra Part I, note 2.
5. Hockett, *Capital Commons*, supra Part I, note 2. See generally Alan Meltzer, *A History of the Federal Reserve*, Volumes 1 and 2 (2004–2010).
6. See sources cited id.
7. Id. We'll come back to this oddity below.
8. An evocative history of the period is Ron Chernow, *The House of Morgan: An American Banking Dynasty and the Rise of Modern Finance* (2010). See also Hockett, *Capital Commons*, supra Part I, note 2; and Meltzer, supra note 5.
9. Id.
10. Id. See also Robert Hockett, 'Save Europe's Marriage with a Trial Separation,' *Reuters*, June 12, 2012; and Robert Hockett, 'What the Euro's Troubles Really Mean,' *The Hill*, July 4, 2014.
11. Id.
12. Id. See also Herbert Croly, *The Promise of American Life* (1909); and Herbert Croly, *Progressive Democracy* (1914). Croly, incidentally, who co-founded the *New Republic* with Walter Lippmann and the Progressive movement with his friends and associates Louis Brandeis, Felix Frankfurter, Learned Hand, and Theodore Roosevelt, is a particularly interesting figure in the present connection—and not only for his having anticipated by nearly a century the present author's calls for a Hamiltonian-Jeffersonian synthesis in American policy and programmatics. For he also eventually worked his way, on the basis of those very (small 'r' republican) values, to advocacy of another key aim of the present author's work – that of a much wider-spread employee ownership of their own firms. See again Hockett, *A Republic of Producers*, supra Part I, note 2.
13. Id.
14. Id.

15. Id.
16. Id.
17. See again supra note 12 and sources cited supra, note supra Part I, note 2.
18. Hockett, *Capital Commons*, supra Part I, note 2.
19. See sources cited supra note 12.
20. Id. Also Hockett, *Rousseauvian Money*, supra note 2.
21. Id.

CHAPTER 3

Central Banking with (More) Centralization: The Breakdown of the 1913 Compromise and the Productive-Republican Fed

Abstract This chapter tells the tale of the demise of the 1913 Fed and its replacement by the Fed of today in preliminary, summary fashion in order to facilitate understanding of the more detailed, theoretically informed treatment of the subsequent chapters. The 1913 understanding of the RBD, this chapter indicates, was strong on endogenous money and hence productive allocation, but was weak on exogenous money and hence stable modulation—matters which didn't assume continuously 'existential' import until the modern era with its ever-tighter integration of separate regional and international credit and money markets. This in turn led to the doctrine's unfortunate wholesale 'discrediting' after the financial dramas of the later 1920s and early 1930s. The failure here, we find, was experienced by both Fed and Congressional policymakers as traumatic and confidence-killing. It thus led to an over-correction—in this case a frantic abandonment of the RBD altogether, rather than replacing its then 'Strong' formulation with the 'Weak' formulation I give it below. Though this change aided in the task of modulating *exogenous* money aggregates, it could not actually solve the *full* modulation problem without continuing to attend to the productive (not speculative) *allocation* of *endogenous* money aggregates as the original, pre-1935 Fed had done. That is then what the next Part of the Book endeavors to show.

R. C. Hockett, *Spread the Fed*,
https://doi.org/10.1007/978-3-031-72051-2_3

Keywords Banking · Banking Act of 1935 · Booms · Busts · Central Banking · Credit · Depressions · Dollar · Elastic Currency · Endogenous Money · Exogenous Money · Fed District Banks · Federal Open Market Committee · Federal Reserve System · First World War · Fisher · FOMC · Glass · Gold Standard · Panics · Productivism · Productivist Central Banking · Productive-Republicanism · Real Bills Doctrine · Republicanism · Speculation · Warburg · War Debt · War Reparations

Within a few years of the Fed's founding in 1913, its 'distributed' character began to come under a certain degree of stress. First came the First World War, which required a productive mobilization that in its turn required greater financial concentration and counterinflationary vigilance.

President Wilson established a War Industries Board and a complementary War Finance Corporation to do the lion's share of the planning, producing, distributing and financing across the entire nation in this connection.[1] But the Fed and the Treasury were of necessity recruited into the concerted national effort—in particular, to modulate credit aggregates so as to tamp down the inflationary pressures inevitably generated by wartime spending. They accordingly had to become ever more national, not merely regional, in orientation.[2]

They also grew more inventive, in ways that would yield significant nationwide consequences where both public and private finance were concerned. Pursuant to its complementary war finance role, for example, Treasury developed many of the taxation and capital market activities that are most familiar to us today—not to mention, indirectly, Congress's later abused 'debt ceiling' legislation in response.[3] And pursuant to *its* complementary war finance and money-modulatory role, the Fed in this period invented one of the principal practices that, once 'privatized' later, would morph into a notoriously destabilizing form of 'shadow banking'—namely, the repo transaction.[4]

After the First World War came both a national pandemic—the so-called 'Spanish Flu' of 1918–19—and, after that, a suddenly booming national economy and bubbling mortgage and stock markets. These stemmed both from 'pent up' consumer demand and from massively grown wartime industrial capacity converted to peacetime production to satisfy it.[5]

While Fed, Treasury, and other public officials grew increasingly worried over the financial froth that accompanied the booming 'real' economy, sharp-eyed financiers developed ever more creative means of extending, then packaging and selling, both consumer and real estate credit, than ever more speculative credit.[6] It accordingly grew steadily more apparent that much more centralized oversight and control over our evermore free-flowing national credit supply would be a systemic necessity.

As seems nearly always to happen, however, none of these worries or attendant imperatives came to much until after the dreaded calamity that fueled them had actually occurred and thus vindicated them. The process of fully centralizing our central bank accordingly came to rough completion only after the crash of 1929 and ensuing Great Depression. But completion of a sort did come, in the form of a battery of New Deal reforms, a remarkably large fraction of which focused on banking, central banking, and centralized national money modulation.[7] These understandably focused the Fed on what I above named the money-*modulatory* task, which is inherently national (even transnational), not merely regional in scope.

In the capital market subsector of the financial sector, for example, Congress enacted a new set of regulatory requirements administered by a new regulator—the Securities and Exchange Commission (SEC)—in the name not merely of financial consumer protection, as remarkably many today seem mistakenly to believe, but of macroprudential money modulation.[8] In the nexus between the capital market and *banking* sectors, in turn, Congress aimed through the Glass-Steagall Act to end the flow of indefinitely extensible, endogenously generated credit-money from banks—thanks to their de facto Fed franchise role, the principal source of that public 'resource'—into speculative secondary and tertiary securities and derivatives markets, as distinguished from the productive primary markets focused on the 'real' economy.[9]

On the banking and hence central banking side of the market/institution divide the reforms were yet more transformative. They set the Fed on a seemingly irrevocable course toward full centralization. The Federal Open Market Committee (FOMC), for example, which gave pride of place to the Fed Board and New York's Regional Fed while rotating the remainder of its seats across other Regional Feds, was established just over two decades after enactment of the Federal Reserve Act itself by the Banking Act of 1935. This was a means of tightening federal monetary control and thereby preventing a repeat of the financially volatile 1920s that had culminated in 1929's crash.[10]

Only a bit less directly, the Federal Deposit Insurance Act of 1933 had introduced not only a form of depositor confidence support—which, like consumer protection in the case of the securities laws, surprisingly many appear to assume is deposit insurance's sole purpose—but also yet another new regulator, the Federal Deposit Insurance Corporation ('FDIC,' 'the Corporation'), charged with bank leverage regulation. The Corporation, right from the get-go, worked in tandem with the Fed to lever insurance conditionality into a means by which to assert federal macroprudential control over not merely national and other Fed-Member-, but now also state-chartered non-Member banks.[11]

The FDIC's primary regulatory role, again as seemingly overlooked by remarkably many observers, reveals quite clearly its macroprudential money-modulatory purpose.[12] I refer to the capital-, that is to say, leverage regulatory regime it administers.[13] To regulate bank leverage is to regulate bank credit, and to regulate bank credit is to regulate 'bank money,' a.k.a. 'credit money,' which of course constitutes by far the lion's share of the national money supply.[14] The incorporation of countercyclical pricing into the Deposit Insurance system earlier in the present century of course simply underscores the point.[15]

Conditioning FDIC insurance on bank compliance with FDIC-administered capital rules was accordingly a mode of completing federal control over the nation's money supply, particularly given the FDIC's regular collaboration with the Fed.[16] In time, however, even this conditionality-based form of federal assertion proved unnecessary, as Congress subjected even state-chartered non-Member banks *directly* to our Fed-administered *liquidity*-regulatory—that is, its 'reserve requirement'—regime nationwide.[17]

In effect, then, our national money's evolution from (a) what I above called non-uniform, privately-issued 'wildcat' currencies constantly fluctuating in value relative both to goods and services and to one another, through (b) a uniform Treasury-issued 'Greenback' currency fluctuating in value only relative to goods and services, on down to (c) an elastic Fed-issued currency whose supply could be modulated to maintain stable value even relative to goods and services, not just other monies, was more or less than completed.[18] There remained some fine-tuning to be done—ultimately in the form of a more *forthrightly* 'macroprudential' style of regulation of the financial system as a whole, through the post-2008 Dodd-Frank Act—but in essentials the requisite institutional infrastructure was by the 1940s in place.[19]

Variations across regions in the practice of monetizing bills of exchange and other forms of commercial paper, along with other lending forms, in consequence also narrowed over these decades.[20] For some of these practices, owing to an overly crude form of the RBD as we'll detail below, had turned up as culprits in both the real estate finance abuses and the capital market excesses that had generated the market bubble that burst in 1929.[21] In part all of these post-1929 changes simply reflected a less and less variegated, even though still at least somewhat heterogeneous, national economy.[22] But in part they also reflected the growing necessity of unified 'systemic' money modulation and financial regulation as accelerating trans-regional financial *integration* amplified both the potential for, and the consequences of, nationwide financial *contagion*.[23]

What they all meant for our central bank's structure and primary preoccupations, though, was that the Fed predictably grew ever more 'northeastern' in its attentions. The principal institutions in *need* of close monitoring in the name of national monetary stability were located in Boston and, especially, New York City.[24]

A similar regulatory 'spurt' to that of the 1930s some seventy-five years later, in response to a cross-*sectoral* integration of finance fully counterpart to the trans-*regional* integration of money that had occurred prior to 1929, brought further consolidation of the 1930s form.[25] I refer to the Dodd-Frank response to that other 'Great' financial calamity, the Great Recession of the early 2010s. Here the financial integration that necessitated greater regulatory and money-modulatory integration nationwide was at least as much a response to *functional* integration in financial services (think 'shadow banking'), which had flowed past much of the leftover 1930s regime, as it was to further *national* integration of one highly systemically important subsector of that sector—*mortgage* finance.[26]

In the end, then, especially after the financial dramas of the Great Depression and Great Recession eras, the Fed Board and Federal Reserve Bank of New York had, in some collaboration with the FDIC, by 2016 fully emerged both as 'first among equals' where national monetary and financial policy were concerned, and even as 'central bank to the world,' more or less, where crisis management in an ever more integrated *global* financial system was concerned.[27] A more integrated economy had brought more integrated governance—and hence ever more centralized 'central *banking*.'[28]

Notes

1. Id. See also Robert Hockett, 'The U.S. Must Take Equity Stakes in the Companies it Rescues,' *Financial Times*, March 28, 2020; Robert Hockett, 'The U.S. Must Ramp Up Production by the World Wars I & II Playbook, not the 2008 Playbook,' *Business Insider*, March 29, 2020; Robert Hockett, 'We Are at War and Need Wartime Institutions to Keep Our Economy Afloat,' *The Hill*, April 4, 2020.
2. See sources cited id. Also Hockett, sources cited supra Chapter 2, note 20.
3. Id. See Also Robert Hockett & Daniel Alpert, 'The Budget is Its Own Debt Ceiling,' *Reuters*, October 10, 2013.
4. Id.
5. See Robert Hockett & Daniel Dillon, *Income Inequality and Market Fragility 2: The Model Applied*, 63 Challenge 35 (2019).
6. Id.
7. Hockett, *Capital Commons*, supra Part I, note 2. Even a casual look at FDR's presidential campaign posters of 1936 shows how many of the first term accomplishments in which the President took pride were banking and finance-regulatory reforms. See also Robert Hockett, *A Fixer-Upper for Finance*, 87 Wash. U. L. Rev. 1213 (2009).
8. See Robert Hockett, *The Macroprudential Significance of the Securities Laws* (working paper, 2014), available at [link]. The Glass-Steagall separation of commercial from investment banking, for example, was not just about protecting 'other people's money,' held in commercial bank deposits, from speculators. It was at least as much about preventing depository institutions, which are able to generate endogenous credit-money with abandon, from directing that money in ways that generated hyperinflation in secondary asset markets. Id. See also Hockett, *A Fixer-Upper for Finance*, supra note 7. And cf. Hockett, *Finance without Financiers*, supra Chapter 2, note 2.
9. See sources cited id.

10. See Hockett, *Macroprudential Significance*, supra note 8; Hockett, *A Fixer-Upper*, supra Chapter 2, note 2. See also Robert Hockett, *The Macroprudential Turn: From Institutional 'Safety and Soundness' to Systemic 'Financial Stability' in Finance and Its Regulation*, 9 Va. L. & Bus. Rev. 201 (2014).
11. See sources cited id.
12. Id.
13. Id.
14. Id.
15. Id.
16. Id.
17. Id.
18. See again Hockett, *Capital Commons*, supra Part I, note 2; Hockett, *Money's Past is Fintech's Future*, supra Part I, note 8; Menand, *Monetary Basis*, supra Part I, note 8.
19. See again Hockett, *Macroprudential Significance*, supra note 8; Hockett, *A Fixer-Upper*, supra Chapter 2, note 2; and Hockett, *Macroprudential Turn*, supra note 10.
20. Id.
21. Id.
22. Hockett, *Capital Commons*, supra Part I, note 2.
23. Id. Also Hockett, *Macroprudential Significance*, supra note 8; Hockett, *A Fixer-Upper*, supra Chapter 2, note 2; and Hockett, *Macroprudential Turn*, supra note 10.
24. See sources cited id.
25. Id.
26. Id.
27. See, e.g., Robert Hockett, *Bretton Woods 1.0: An Essay in Constructive Retrieval*, 16 NYU J. Legis. & Pub. Pol'y 401 (2013); An Essay in Constructive Retrieval, Robert Hockett, 'Is the Fed Jimmy Stewart? Is It the World's Central Bank?,' *Benzinga*, Dec. 4, 2010; & Robert Hockett, 'Global Currency Relations, Macroeconomic Recovery, and Long Term Financial Stability, *Benzinga*, Nov. 18, 2010.

28 See again Hockett, *Capital Commons*, supra Part I, note 2; and Hockett, *Rousseauvian Money*, supra Chapter 2, note 2.

PART II

Central Banking's Early 'Operating System': The Real Bills Doctrine

We're now at last situated to look more carefully at (a) the 'theory' upon which our Fed—and indeed most if not all central banks—operated in the early modern era of central banking, and at (b) the 'theory' it acts upon now. We've encountered these theories already in the brief histories recounted above, but must now consider them in greater detail—in order both to understand their strengths and weaknesses and, in that light, to develop at an optimal 'operating system' for a form of central banking in synch with our Productive-Republican ideals.

As noted above, both the 1913 and 1935 Fed 'operating systems' have been exactly half-right, with full 'righteousness' to be found solely in their synthesis. That of course is the project of this Book, and the vision of the Book's 'restorative renewal' plans in Part III. It is in that spirit that we turn now to our Fed's ups and downs in more theoretic detail.

We can 'get into' the proverbial 'weeds' most gracefully, I think, by this time, unlike above, operating in historical reverse—that is, by starting with where we are now in the realm of central banking theory, then re-running the history recounted above with a view to the premises underlying contemporary understanding. Central to current thinking, of course, is the notion of central bank 'independence.' So it will be convenient to start there, attending carefully to the premises on which this oft-declared, seldom understood ideal rests. Believe it or not, this will then take us to both what went wrong, and what was just fine, in our first Fed's rendition of the RBD.

The ideal of central bank 'independence' seems often to be extolled or decried in an untethered, free-floating manner. This sometimes occasions unnecessary confusion. Calls by some—including some of my academic and Fed colleagues and friends—to 'end independence' and 'democratize the Fed' several years back, for example, apparently mean that the Fed should be more answerable to Congress. Yet it seemed not to have occurred to some of the aforementioned, while they are on this roll, that the White House and Congress often are in the hands of a political faction that routinely garners many millions fewer votes in national elections than does their rival party. If you want to democratize the Fed, I have thus often suggested, you might want to start by democratizing the U.S.—or at least the White House and Congress.

You see the point. Central bank independence cannot really be *understood* in institutional isolation any more than central banks can themselves *operate* in institutional isolation. In ordinary usage the word 'independent' is implicitly, when not explicitly, followed by a preposition. It is a relative, 'unsaturated' predicate, indexed by some assumed 'independent variable' *from* which or *of* which various values of the dependent variable—'independence' of one sort or another—are variably dependent or independent. And there are *many* independent variables in relation to which we *might* unreflectively be taking the 'independence' in question dependently to vary. Do we mean 'independent of' the executive of a national government? Independent of' the legislature? Independent of 'the democratic process' or 'the political process' more generally? Independent of *what*, exactly?

Even once we decide which independent variable(s) we have in mind, moreover, we face yet further requirements of yet further specification of the *dependent variable itself* before we know what we are talking about. Do we mean 'complete' independence (in some sense) from what the bank is meant to be independent of, under all circumstances always and everywhere? Do we mean independence only in respect of certain decisions or subject matters, and/or within certain time or event intervals—for example, only as to interest rate targets, workforce participation rates, wealth gaps, environmental impacts ... or within political campaign cycles, 'staggered' across campaign cycles, outside of financial crises, or ... again, *what*?

Without more refinement, it's not clear we are talking about anything at all when we talk about central bank 'independence.'

As critical as further specification along all of these broad lines is to productive discussion of central bank independence, however, it is a somewhat narrower range of context-relativity *within* this large ambit that needs highlighting in this Part, Part II. We must talk about central bank independence as it figures into a specific set of institutional assumptions that most current discussions of the subject seem to assume as background conditions. We can foreground and sympathetically critique this set of assumptions, *accepting* them in part while also *rejecting* them in part, to arrive at a richer understanding of central bank theory and practice first from 1913 to 1935, then from 1935 to the present.

There is, we shall see, an existing institution-bound 'thought-complex' in which most, if not all, present-day discussions of central bank independence are implicitly embedded. This complex is partly but not wholly sound, and can be made fully sound only through careful identification and explication, critical examination, and purposeful reconstruction.

Reconstructing the relevant thought-complex is what we shall do in this Part of the Book. In the end, we shall find that one principal assumption upon which most, if not all, contemporary discussions of central bank independence tacitly rely—namely, that central banks must and do engage only in what I long ago dubbed neutral 'modulation,' not what I dubbed inherently contestable 'allocation,' of endogenous Wicksellian credit-money—is false. So, we shall find, is the associated assumption that central bank *allocation* cannot be done *neutrally* or, therefore, incontestably and hence in a legitimately independent manner. At least this is so, as we'll see, where the only forms of neutrality, good faith contestability, and 'independence' we should care about in a would-be democratic productive-republic are in play.

The implications of these conclusions will prove 'radical,' in the original Latin sense of the term. They are foundational and far-reaching where sound public allocation of the public's own investment capital—its central-bank-issued credit-money—is concerned. They reconstitute and recombine the roles of individual and collective action in the realm of finance and, therefore, *production*. They yield, in other words, the normative restoration-cum-reform plan that is this Book's ultimate object.

Let us then turn now to examining in more detail what I suggested above about the Fed's 'operating system'—the Real Bills Doctrine and the analytic distinctions upon which it rests. We'll start with the latter, then turn to the former.

CHAPTER 4

Theoretic Foundations: Scissors Require Two Blades—Endogenous Money, Its Modulation, and Its Allocation

Abstract This Chapter begins with Part II by laying out the fundamentals of endogenous credit-money and the combined allocative and modulatory functions that endogeneity presses upon any central bank or monetary authority. All bank credit denominated as legal tender by a public sector payments system like that of the U.S. and other 'developed' economy jurisdictions, the Chapter shows, is endogenously generated by lending decisions made by publicly licensed banking or cognate lending institutions. The only limits upon such lending are banks' profit opportunities, determined by those seeking credit, and whatever strictures are publicly imposed in the name of liquidity and solvency assurance. The Chapter then shows how the Fed's founders at least implicitly understood these features of money and the central bank functions that they necessitated. This, the Chapter shows, was reflected in their acceptance of the RBD. It also is hardly surprising, as eighteenth- and nineteenth-century observers in both the markets and the academy alike—from John Law through James Steuart and Adam Smith down through Leon Walras and Knut Wicksell—seem uniformly to have held far more nuanced understandings of credit and money than did the purveyors of what became orthodoxy during the twentieth century.

Keywords Banks · Central Banking · Bubbles · Busts · Collective Action Problems · Credit · Discounting · Dollar · Elastic Currency ·

R. C. Hockett, *Spread the Fed*,
https://doi.org/10.1007/978-3-031-72051-2_4

Endogenous Money · Exogenous Money · Federal Reserve System · Federal Open Market Committee · Fisher · FOMC · Glass · Great Depression · Law · Marx · Monetary Policy · Necessary Conditions · Panics · Productivism · Productivist Central Banking · Real Bills Doctrine · Recursive Collective Action Problems · Smith · Speculation · Steuart · Sufficient Conditions · Walras · Warburg · Wicksell · Strong RBD · Weak RBD

Where public finance in a decentralized exchange economy with endogenous credit-money is concerned (more on that phrase below), there are two broad public functions that have to be collectively discharged. This is so notwithstanding—indeed, even because of—contemporary market exchange's primarily decentralized, 'privately ordered' character. People seem never explicitly to say—or perhaps even to recognize—this. But they implicitly assume it every time they speak of 'monetary' and 'fiscal' policy, or of 'central banks' and 'finance ministries,' as legitimate yet distinct functions and institutions of public governance, respectively.

The first such function is what I've long been calling the money-*modulatory* task, while the second is what I've been calling the money-*allocative* task. These tasks are seldom identified, let alone named. They go, in effect, barely noticed because at best only tacitly assumed. Partly for this very reason, I suspect, what goes yet more crucially unnoticed is ***(a) that these two functions both are necessitated by credit-money's endogeneity itself, and (b) that this same endogeneity renders the functions both theoretically and operationally inseparable.***

The modulatory and allocative functions accordingly constitute, we might say, two blades of one scissors of public finance. I'll elaborate and explain in a moment. But first a bit more on money endogeneity and the blades individually, along with their relations to the ideology of central bank independence and what below I'll identify as recursive collective action predicaments. For only when we are fully clear on the blades' purposes and operational environments can we grasp their full functional inseparability.

4.1 Endogenous Central Bank Credit-Money: Publicly Generated, Privately Allocated Investment Capital

Crucial to all I've said thus far and all that I'll say below is one crucial feature of money in any fractional reserve or other bona fide banking system—its endogeneity. I and others, from John Law to Adam Smith and Karl Marx on down through Leon Walras and Knut Wicksell have written extensively on bank credit-money's endogenous character elsewhere, so there is no need to be tedious here. The essentials, however, must be grasped firmly to understand the modulo-allocative inseparability that I am at pains to explicate in this Chapter. So here they are in a few paragraphs...

Contemporary polities publicly license private sector banks and other financial institutions to generate and allocate national credit-money supplies without falling foul of anti-counterfeiting laws. This they do by (a) authorizing these institutions to extend spendable credit in fiduciary account form (the credit feature of credit-money), while (b) publicly 'recognizing' payments made out of such accounts as discharging commercial obligations via legal tender laws and associated public administration of national payments systems (the monetary feature of credit-money).

This amounts to public outsourcing of the public's own money-issuance authority to private sector lending institutions, presumably on the (dubious) theory that they are in all cases better at productive allocation than is the public sector. Hence Wicksell's (1896) dubbing this money-form 'bank money,' which we generalize to issuance by additional financial institutions through use of the broader term 'credit-money.'

There are three characteristics of endogenous Wicksellian credit-money to emphasize for present purposes. First, it represents by far the greater portion of contemporary economies' 'money supplies.' Second, the only limitation on this form of money's generation by private sector institutions, apart from public guidance (more on which below), is the prospective profitability of lending—a prospective profitability that in stratified financial markets (more on which presently) includes, crucially, loans not just for legitimately macroeconomy-growing *productive* purposes, but also for macroeconomically destabilizing speculative *gambling* purposes. And third, owing to the dispositive role played by *public authority* in enabling this form of credit to function as money at all, Wicksellian credit-money is effectively *public investment capital.*

Publicly licensed, yet private-profit-actuated, endogenous credit-money extension just is publicly issued, yet privately allocated, investment capital. *In this very hybridity of contemporary investment capital lies the inseparability of credit modulation and allocation as essential public functions.*

4.2 First Blade of the Scissors: Modulation, Technocracy, & 'Independence'

Now, what I call public finance's *modulatory* task is *straightforwardly* necessitated by the aforementioned endogeneity of credit-money. It is the task of retaining variable money-quantity fluctuations, rooted in the indefinite extensibility and contractibility of bank-issued credit, within a tolerable band. In finance parlance, this is a *collaring* function.

Variable credit-money availability, made possible by money endogeneity, opens the door to aggregate over- or under-extension of credit relative to goods, services, and (euphemism alert) financial 'asset' quantities purchasable with credit-money. This in turn renders credit-fueled inflation, hyperinflation, deflation, and Fisherian debt-deflation ever-present dangers.

Because credit-money endogeneity *also* renders inflations and deflations potentially *self-worsening without limit*—amplifying them into what I long ago christened *recursive collective action problems* (more on which below)—*centralized management* of endogenous credit-money supplies is imperative if decentralized market finance, and with it decentralized market exchange (including in production- input markets) generally, is to be sustained over time. Money supply management is, accordingly, one minimal degree of *centralized* jurisdiction that must be retained if otherwise *decentralized* market exchange is to be possible at all over time.

That bears repeating in production-focused form: *Continued private ordering of production requires, at a minimum, a high degree of public ordering of finance.* (This is the message of my *Capital Commons* and *Wealth of Our Commonwealth.*) And what goes overlooked as we shall soon see, this means public *allocation* nearly as much as it means public *modulation*.

Now the populations of many contemporary polities seem at least partly or semi-consciously aware of the public modulatory imperative. For they all exercise some degree of modulatory *collective agency* where endogenous credit-money supplies are concerned. (My argument below is that they will have to exercise more.)

They do so through public instrumentalities tellingly labeled '*central* banks' or 'monetary *authorities*,' the italicized components of these phrases suggest collective agency and corresponding centralizations of authority. Polities then task these instrumentalities with collaring price fluctuations by modulating supplies and circulation-velocities of endogenous credit-money relative to that which money exchanges for or commands—again, goods, services, production-inputs, and 'assets.'

Now comes a crucial move in the modern central bank thought-complex I'm reconstructing. The modulatory task as I have just characterized it is inherently *counter-majoritarian*, in what lawyers will recognize as the Bickelian sense, as a theoretical matter. And it is inherently *technical*, in a straightforward sense, as a practical matter. And this is the justification, fully appreciated or not, of modern central banks' 'independent' and 'technocratic' characters alike, in the senses that celebrants and critics alike seem to have in mind.

The modulatory task is counter-*majoritarian* because it has to be counter-*cyclical* within any environment of decentralized market exchange. It has to be counter-cyclical in turn because it is rooted in inflation's and deflation's character as endogeneity-rooted *recursive collective action problems*, in the sense just noted, in any such environment. Here's what I mean...

4.3 Endogeneity's Achilles Heel: Recursive Collective Action Problems ('ReCAPs')

A collective action problem is of course simply a choice situation in which multiple individually rational decisions aggregate into collectively irrational outcomes. It is accordingly 'tragic' in the classical Greek ('damned if you do, damned if you don't') sense of the word. 'Commons tragedies,' 'bums' rushes,' arms races, and 'positional goods arms races' are all varyingly familiar cases in point. A recursive such problem (or what I abbreviate as a 'ReCap') is just such a tragedy as self-worsening through iterated decisions, with each decision at time t informed by and responding to the outcomes of decisions at time t-1.

Examples of ReCaps abound in decentralized goods, banking, and capital markets. A few familiar examples will make the point ...

Inflation: You and I see prices rising, and hence rationally buy more now rather than waiting till later; but this just makes prices rise faster.
Deflation: You and I see prices falling, and hence rationally defer buying and hiring till later; but this just makes prices fall further and unemployment rise faster.
Bank Run: You and I hear that our bank is faced with liquidity trouble, hence rationally head there to withdraw our funds; but this simply hastens the eventuality we fear.
Asset Price Bubble: Simply a hyper-inflation in financial markets.
Market Crash or *Asset 'Fire Sale'*: Simply a debt-deflation or 'bank run' on assets.
And so on ...

The stratification, derivation, and financialization developments noted above to be naturally recurring phenomena under decentralized financial arrangements stem from the recursive mechanisms that underlie ReCaps. They also give full play to the mechanisms through which speculation comes steadily to displace productive investment in market economies where finance is as decentralized as production. For a market in claims at stratum $n + 1$ upon claims at stratum n is precisely what enables betting—speculating—directly on price movements at stratum n—price movements that need not solely, and certainly do not directly, reflect success or otherwise in production at 'ground level' (stratum $n = 0$). And financial recursion just is the repetitive iteration of this form of betting.

Betting of this kind from the point of view of those seeking to hedge at any stratum n is effectively the attempt to re-socialize—to 'spread,' or 'share'—the risks that attend either productive activity or lower-stratum (n-m, with $m > 0$) bets on productive activity when these risks are individually borne, which in this (decentralized production) context they are by definition. Financial intermediation and derivation, hence stratification and financialization, are simply the natural, collectively irrational (because counter-productive) upshot of these individually rational efforts.

Markets in which endogenous publicly generated, privately allocated credit-money figures as a medium of exchange are rife with predicaments of this sort—a fact that continues to go surprisingly unremarked. In an inflation or hyperinflation (a.k.a. 'bubble'), for example, individuals rationally buy now in anticipation of prices rising later. In so doing they collectively drive prices yet higher, leading to more purchasing, more price rises, and so on. In a deflation or bank-run or 'bust,' the same happens in reverse once the credit that's fueled the upswing is exhausted in what is frequently labeled an 'inflection point.'

In all such cases, individual agents collectively and indeed tragically drive collectively irrational cycles simply by making individually rational decisions. Only a collective agent, acting in the name of all, can prevent such decisions from aggregating into collectively irrational outcomes. This the agent does by short-circuiting the recursion cycle itself—crucially, by *countering the crowd*, by 'acting contrarian.' More specifically, the agent does so by rendering participation in the relevant 'crowd' no longer individually rational—for example, by raising borrowing costs, by taxing away asset price capital gains, by taxing speculative 'short swing' or 'churning' transactions, or the like. The aim is to close the spreads between low credit costs and rising goods, services, or 'asset' prices.

It is easy to see why some degree of insulation from crowd preferences—some form and degree of 'independence'—will be necessary if this contrarian task of counter-cyclical collective agency is to be discharged effectively. Counter-majoritarian action is possible only when short-term majoritarian preferences can be temporarily disregarded, hence when democratic accountability is 'lagged' rather than immediate.

Here, then, is the 'independence' piece of the modulatory task. The 'technocratic' bit enters through what is required to discharge the role not so much *at all*, as *competently and effectively*. Central banks have to modulate endogenous money supplies relative to anticipated resources, goods, services, and asset supplies that money purchases. This involves massive data collection, aggregation, estimation, and prediction. So does the task of deploying the tools used to vary credit-money availability relative to those projections. These are technical tasks in which technical expertise, though not *sufficient* to discharge the task, is in any event necessary.

4.4 Second Blade of the Scissors: Allocation, Democracy, & 'Accountability'

Now for the *allocative* task. Here we speak less in 'quantitative' than in what might be called 'qualitative' terms where endogenous credit-money is concerned. We are foregrounding not 'how much' or 'how fast' money is flowing or changing hands so much as 'where' it is flowing. The first question to ask about allocation is whether and why it is really an objective of public finance at all. Is collective agency as obviously necessary here as it is in the case of modulation?

It takes some, but not much, reflection to see that the answer has to be yes. Polities do things and act on decisions about what shall collectively be done. That is indeed all that collective agency and collective action themselves are—decisions made and executed jointly by or on behalf of multiple deciders acting 'as one,' be the 'one' a family or other association, a business, or a tribe, community, or nation-state. What anyone does—public officers and other collective agents included—in turn always involves some use of resources. And, again in any monetary exchange economy such as our own, this in turn requires the commanding of resources through money expenditures.

But this just is allocation. It is money-allocation for purposes of resource-use in pursuit of public objectives.

Polities and other associations also typically take interest, for purposes of maintaining some degree of social or juridical cohesion if not actual justice, in distributions of advantage and disadvantage among their constituent members. This too just is an interest in resource allocation, with 'resources' now understood broadly as materials used, not now by publics in pursuit of public objectives, but by private citizens and sub-sovereign associations of citizens in pursuit of privately conceived plans and projects.

Now because resource-, including money-, allocation produces comparative 'winners and losers' in connection with literally every decision, polities actuated by democratic values will tend to view the allocative character of particular subjects of collective decision as best subject to democratic *accountability*. The apocryphal war cry of the American Revolution—'no taxation without representation'—is but one dramatic example of the idea at work here. We accordingly tend to vest the more *overtly* money-allocative authority of our polity in institutions that we endeavor to keep less technocratic and insulated, more democratic and accountable.

We resort, in other words, to legislatures subject to regular elections, and to finance ministries subject in turn to continuous legislative oversight. Here, again with varying cognizance of the fact, is the basis for contemporary jurisdictions' maintaining finance ministries or treasuries separate from their central banks and other monetary authorities. Here also, accordingly, is the basis for running aspirationally separate 'fiscal' and 'monetary' policies via these institutions, with each institution issuing its own monetary or quasi-monetary financial instruments in furtherance of its mission (*Federal Reserve* Notes or '*dollar* bills' in the one case, for example, and *Treasury* Notes, Bills, or Bonds in the other).

The idea, implicit or otherwise, is that the one institution will only neutrally *modulate* supplies of, and accordingly be authorized to issue, explicitly monetary instruments and their fiduciary (e.g., bank account) equivalent. The other institution will instead overtly *allocate* and accordingly be able to monetize only such of its own financial instruments as the legislature authorizes for particular purposes and the 'independent' central bank or public will purchase to convert into spendable money. Et voila, central bank independence and finance ministry accountability in modern public finance.

4.5 Scissors Need Two Blades: No Effective Modulation without Sound Allocation

Now, even *granting* the *intuitive* tractability and *provisional* usefulness for some purposes of (a) the modulation/allocation distinction as just elaborated, and (b) its modern institutional embodiment, recent events confront us with a set of questions that we can either duck, as we have done for five decades now, or instead finally address. The questions are: (1) Is the modulation/allocation distinction as crisp as I have just made it sound? (2) Has it always been strictly *observed*, tacitly or otherwise? And (3) if it isn't or hasn't, are the thought-complex that latently and therefore uncritically relies upon the distinction, and that complex's current institutional embodiment, salvageable?

I think the answer to the first two queries is no while that to the third query is yes—with revision. That is, the distinction partly dissolves under scrutiny and has often been at least tacitly rejected, at least in part and for brief periods, in consequence. But it also is partly salvageable if we attend carefully to its actual contours and respond institutionally by reconstructing our principal organs of public finance—our central banks and finance ministries. And, crucially, *this need not imply any objectionable form of non-neutrality or, therefore, 'independence.'* My reasons for saying these things are rooted in the very phenomenon that leads us to recognize the urgency of the modulatory task itself—again, credit-money endogeneity.

Credit-money's endogeneity, which necessitates modulation as a *necessary* collective function in the first place, also renders effective modulation *impossible* absent a certain definable range of forthright collective *allocation*—a range I'll define momentarily in principled fashion. And this means that more thoroughgoing fiscal and monetary coordination or consolidation—independence's partial contrary—which always intensifies during crises but then recedes once the crises appear to be past, must become a 'new normal.' At least that is so if ever-deeper, more frequent, and more devastating crises are not *themselves* to remain a new normal.

Here's what I mean...

Credit-fueled bubbles develop as over-issuances of speculative credit-money to traders who spot and then trade upon fads-in-the-making. The objects of these fads can be virtually anything—'junk' this, 'subprime' that, 'crypto' whatever...

Once a 'boom' in such objects begins to attract (euphemism alert) 'momentum traders,' a decentralized monetary exchange economy with endogenous credit-money and 'deep' secondary financial and tertiary derivatives markets—what I elsewhere dub 'stratified,' or 'meta-' markets—generates the most formidable of all known recursive collective action predicaments: the credit-fueled asset price bubble and subsequent bust. For indefinitely extensible credit can be borrowed cheaply to purchase 'assets' whose prices are rising at rates higher than borrowing rates—a transaction type that for a while will be profitable for lender and borrower alike.

Under boom conditions of this sort it becomes individually rational for 'investors' (euphemism alert) to borrow in order to buy in order either (a) to sell on the secondary markets or (b) to 'hedge' (euphemism alert) on the tertiary markets. But everyone's acting thus rationally aggregates into irrational, 'runaway train' outcomes as prices are driven to points at which even the most profligate lenders at last balk. Ensuing reversals then culminate in busts as intemperate as their antecedent booms, leaving debt overhang and hence negative net worth in the wake since borrowing costs are fixed while asset prices are variable.

These reactive 'downside' debt-deflations (a.k.a. 'depressions'), which are themselves recursive collective action problems of the same sort, are of course the bane of macroeconomic stability, hence of sustained productive and full-employment activity. *They* must accordingly be defused collectively too. But this is just the modulation challenge that I sketched above, begun in an *allocation* challenge as are all endogenity-rooted modulation challenges.

What then to do? Must all endogenous credit-money *allocation* be 'independently' and 'technocratically' managed just as must *modulation*? Must fiscal and monetary policy be collapsed into one another—fully 'consolidated'? And what then of all of that 'picking of winners and losers,' and of the intolerable 'democratic deficit' that doing this 'technocratically' and 'independently' of politics would seem to entail?

4.6 Production & Speculation: More Distinguishable than Modulation & Allocation

Well, relax. The quandary is not as acute as it looks at first blush. The key is to retrieve a distinction that both (a) is more or less objectively and technically drawable, and (b) used to be routinely technically drawn. We in the U.S. mistakenly abandoned this distinction in 1935 owing to a false lesson drawn from the first years that followed the 1929 crash, but can retrieve it in 'new and improved' form both theoretically and operationally—without even changing our law.

Really? Yes. I am alluding once more to the distinction between *productive* investment and merely *speculative* betting, and the implications of drawing that distinction for how we govern primary investment markets on the one hand, secondary and tertiary betting markets on the other hand.

Start with the distinction itself. While investment and speculation of course overlap at the margin, paradigmatic cases of the former are readily identified cases in which producers and suppliers of material goods and services, or of material inputs to productive processes, are tapping the lending or capital markets. We can call the markets in which all of this happens the 'primary' markets.

Paradigmatic cases of merely speculative betting are cases in which the *claims* generated by primary market investment are *themselves* bought, sold, or bet upon or against, with the speculators borrowing in order to purchase those claims with a view either to selling them at higher prices in secondary markets or capitalizing on such secondary market price changes in other ways through tertiary market derivative instruments. The markets in which these purchases and sales occur are accordingly what I call the 'secondary,' 'tertiary,' and iteratively through time what I call '*n*-ary' or 'meta-' markets. (See again *The Wealth of Our Commonwealth.*)

Primary markets in decentralized exchange economies with endogenous credit-money do not typically generate serious recursive collective action predicaments of the kind that I highlighted above. For they are ultimately 'grounded' in, 'anchored' by, or 'tethered' to, something that nature or physics themselves more or less exogenously modulate—viz., potentially profitable material production. But where credit-money is endogenous and profitability is not immediately tethered to material production but can also include the winning of short-term bets, *meta*-markets have to be *artificially* modulated if there is to be any exogenous constraint upon endogenous credit dissemination.

And this means that modulation will require at least a broad, macro form of allocation—steering money broadly from speculative meta-markets to productive primary markets.

Meanwhile the exogenous modulation in question will still have to be done collectively—both in the manner, and for the reasons, elaborated above. But if the latter is partly allocative, at least as between productive primary markets on the one hand and speculative meta-markets on the other hand, is it politically viable to do that technocratically and 'independently'? Are we faced with yet another 'tragedy' that is the flipside of that tragedy which is the ReCap itself, in the sense that modulation requires independent collective agency while also requiring allocation, which then requires independence-prohibitive *accountable* collective agency?

The answer is no—this needn't be tragic. *For the production/speculation distinction is itself technically tractable and universally appreciable as critical to macroeconomic sustainability (that is, to the avoidance of Marxian 'contradiction' and terminal 'crisis,' while at the same time there is sufficient variety under each heading to allow for a great deal of private ordering where allocation* under *them is concerned.* Hence we can afford a degree of independence to certain forms of central bank allocation and concomitant fiscal-cum-monetary consolidation without (a) resorting to a comprehensive 'state planning' or (b) objectionably insulating the pickers of 'winners and losers' from desirable democratic accountability.

All we need do is keep public capital—again, endogenous central bank credit-money—out of the meta-markets. Let public capital flow only to primary markets, while restricting secondary and tertiary markets solely to pre-accumulated private capital.

We can see how to do this both in early Fed history, prior to the Banking Act of 1935, and in my proposal for an updated version of pre-1935, 'Spread Fed' discounting alike. For more on the former, please start here. And for more on the latter, please start here and here.

CHAPTER 5

The Scissors in Retrospect and Prospect: Real Bills, Real Money, and Reality

Abstract This Chapter lays out in detail the Real Bills Doctrine as understood in Glass's and Warburg's day, along with what was right and what was wrong about that understanding. It emphasizes the early Doctrine's confounding of necessity with sufficiency, dubbing this the crude, 'Strong-Form RBD.' After explaining both what was right and what was wrong with that older rendition, the Chapter develops a more refined, 'Weak-Form RBD,' which I show both to retain what was right about the older form while dispensing with what was wrong in that earlier rendition. The Chapter then shows the Fed's failures of the late 1920s and early 1930s as failures of that earlier, Strong RBD understanding itself, while setting the stage for reforms animated by my more refined 'Weak RBD'—reforms that will restore fully functional, Productivist Central Banking Itself.

Keywords Banks · Central Banking · Bubbles · Busts · Collective Action Problems · Credit · Discounting · Dollar · Elastic Currency · Endogenous Money · Exogenous Money · Federal Reserve System · Federal Open Market Committee · Fisher · FOMC · Glass · Great Depression · Law · Marx · Mints · Monetary Policy · Necessary Conditions · Panics · Productivism · Productivist Central Banking · Real Bills Doctrine · Recursive Collective Action Problems · Rehypothecation · Schumpeter · Smith · Speculation · Steuart ·

R. C. Hockett, *Spread the Fed*,
https://doi.org/10.1007/978-3-031-72051-2_5

Sufficient Conditions · Thornton · Walras · Warburg · Wicksell · Strong RBD · Weak RBD

The founders of the Fed system were at least implicitly aware of what I've laid out in Chapter 4. It is why they adopted a rendition of the RBD and indeed founded the Fed on its basis. They were short-sighted, however, in precisely two ways.

First off, even in the case of endogenous money, the RBD captures reality only absent what I have elsewhere called 'rehypothecation risk,' which means the operation of some analogue to what in finance parlance is known as the 'insurable interest doctrine.' Roughly speaking, whatever underlies the 'real bills' in question must not be multiplied or iteratively monetizable as happens when assets are rehypothecated or when a bet on an 'insured event' can be placed by multiple otherwise-disinterested parties—as when the same goods can be sold and re-sold while the credit instruments that they secure remain outstanding, or when a financial derivative replaces a one-to-one insurance contract enabling millions of people to lay claim to 'compensation' for the same event.[1] I'll explain in more detail below.

And second, even though by far the greater part of most monetary aggregates is endogenous, there can be and often are money sub-aggregates that are exogenous in origin too, particularly in markets where precious metals serve as commodity moneys in the way gold did world-wide until after the Crash of 1929. This, we shall see, proved quite crucial during the Fed's later post-WWI years—years now suggestively known as 'the Roaring 20s' and 'the Great Depression.' It is one thing to be attentive to endogenous money; it is quite another to be *un*aware of *exogenous* money. Sound central banking requires *both* 'baby' *and* 'bathwater.'

The early Fed's 'Strong Form RBD,' spotting allocation's necessity but missing its insufficiency, missed this. The upshot is that the Strong RBD of the early Fed era nicely captured the *necessity* of good allocation to good modulation, but falsely suggested the *sufficiency* of the one for the other as well. This is the error we must now explain and correct.

5.1 The 'Spread' Fed of 1913–1935 and the Strong-Form RBD—Now in Detail

What I have just been saying used to be, perhaps surprisingly, unsurprising. As noted earlier, the founders of the Federal Reserve System in 1913 designed a network of forthrightly allocative regional development finance institutions—the Fed was what I have been calling productively 'spread.' This entailed unabashed cross-regional allocation—much as calls for the Fed to address wealth gaps and climate risk in recent years would do.[2] Each of the twelve regional Federal Reserve District Banks provided short-term funding directly or indirectly (through local banks) to developing businesses that needed it. This they did by 'discounting'—in effect, directly or indirectly purchasing—commercial paper issued by those businesses.

Making Fed lending yet *more* forthrightly allocative were the *eligibility* criteria that the system applied in determining what *kinds* of paper to discount. The Federal Reserve Act was—and ironically remains—quite explicit about this: Fed discount lending is solely for 'productive,' not 'speculative' purposes. The Fed even employed an *index* developed by the World War I era *War Industries Board* (WIB) to assess the 'productivity' of this statutorily mandated 'productive lending,' and housed offices of the WIB's financing arm, the forthrightly allocative War Finance Corporation (WFC), in its regional District Banks to assist with productive development nationwide. You can hardly get more allocative than that.

So what happened? Well, it all boils down to the tragic conflation of necessity with sufficiency identified above—both before and then after the critical year 1935.

The allocative Fed we began with was founded, as we saw, by adherents of the once popular, half-right nineteenth-century rendition of the 'Real Bills Doctrine' (RBD). Prominent among these founders were the aforementioned Paul Warburg and Carter Glass, the latter of Glass-Steagall renown. What I am calling the 'Strong' RBD in its crude nineteenth-century formulation held that so long as the lending of credit-money was kept productive, not speculative, inflation and deflation would be not only less likely, but effectively *impossible*. For the productivity requirement would ensure it remained primary market investment, not meta-market speculation, that money funded.

Yet in fact there are *other* possible sources of monetary disturbance than mere fad investment and meta-market speculation, the effects of which demand-responsive endogenous lending can then procyclically amplify, pursuant to the recursive dynamic described above in connection with what I've dubbed 'ReCAPs,' as readily as if they were the latter. A sudden stoppage of fuel exports by OPEC nations in the 1970s, for example, or a sudden influx of silver into Spain four hundred years earlier, can suddenly alter the money/goods balance, commencing a self-amplifying inflationary or deflationary episode. In effect, exogenous factors can spark endogenous self-amplification.

This is just the general form of the celebrated 'cumulative process' that Thornton noticed in the early, and Wicksell more carefully modeled in the later, nineteenth century—but which Americans tragically didn't take to heart until many decades later when Wicksell was finally translated into English. Something much like it happened in the late 1920s and early 1930s after the twinned real estate and stock market crashes of the 'Roaring 20s.' Exogenous money supply changes stemming from war reparation and debt payments from Europe and Britain were amplified by endogenous lending and contracting before and after 1929, respectively.

What was needed both before and after 1929 was accordingly a countercyclical exogenous tightening, then infusion, first to contract and then to *boost* the by-then only transaction-driven money supply, to *counteract* the *expansion and contraction* in the money supply wrought by the bubble and bust, respectively, and ensuing Fisher-style debt-deflation. But the Fed Board of the time, in thrall to the crude and incomplete, 'Strong Form' rendition of the RBD, judged that the money supply must by definition be adequate to real money demand, and thus took no serious countercyclical corrective action until the proverbial 'horse' had left the proverbial 'barn.' The 'golden fetters' of a still-operative gold standard didn't help in the crisis's early years either.

5.2 The Problem with the ('Strong-Form') RBD as It Stood

Why didn't the Fed's founders, or at least the Fed's personnel, see this? Or: what, more specifically did they miss? As briefly noted above, I think they missed two things: first, the capacity for even 'real bills' to be monetized multiple times through a form of what I above called rehypothecation; and second, the fact that money aggregates can be suddenly changed by exogenous forces additional to endogenous ones. Insofar as they missed these things, their version of the RBD remained what I have been calling the crude, 'Strong-Form' RBD. Had they seen more clearly, they could have formulated a more refined rendition, which I shall formulate fully below and dub '*Refined*,' or 'Weak-Form' RBD.

Let's take the late 1920s and early 1930s Fed's two oversights in turn, then do that reformulating …

As early as the time of Henry Thornton (1845), it was understood that even 'real' bills could be overissued if goods for which the bills paid could be resold before the bills came due.[3] This was so notwithstanding the strengths of the doctrine as advocated by John Law and Adam Smith in the previous century.

Thornton used a simple hypothetical to make his point. Jean-Jacques sells me $100 worth of goods in return for a discountable bill that will come due in twelve months. I in turn sell the $100 worth of goods on to you, also in return for a discountable bill that comes due in twelve months. You then might sell the goods further on in the same manner … and so on. Were sale and resale to occur in this manner, say, once per month, then by the end of one year there could be $1,200 worth of discountable bills in circulation, to which would still correspond only $100 worth of goods.

In itself, this need not be problematic, as with an appropriate discount rate the sum of the time-discounted values of the twelve bills sharing the same re-hypothecated items would come to the price of but one $100 bill held to maturity. But that is the key—that discount rate must be properly chosen and set by some authority, and exercise of this authority is a macro-modulatory, exogenously sourced function. Hence at least this degree of modulatory activity must be engaged in by the central bank or monetary authority even when most credit-money is endogenously generated—unless resale on credit of the kind just imagined, what I'm calling rehypothecation, is rendered somehow impossible. Not to limit it is to invite Thornton's and Wicksell's aforementioned 'cumulative process' of self-feeding inflationary spiral.[4]

Now, insofar as real bills are associated with business plans rather than goods—that is, with things that cannot be resold or rehypothecated—this cumulative process vulnerability does not manifest. And for this reason many—including most nineteenth-century bankers and, later, theorists Lloyd Mints and Joseph Schumpeter—held that the RBD as acted upon in the early twentieth century was in effect 'more right than wrong.' But the important point here is that it *can* go wrong absent recognition of rehypothecation potential—potential that must be exogenously neutralized by an authority able to set and adjust discount rates.

The second vulnerability to which the old Crude-Form RBD was subject, as noted before, was that raised by *exogenous* sources of 'money shock.' Before the late nineteenth century, this danger was muted, as communications technologies were such as to keep global credit markets moving slowly and hence keep exogenous sources of money less prone to rapid ingress and egress. But that changed in the later nineteenth and especially early twentieth centuries. Moreover, the U.S.' role first as chief creditor, then as 'game-changing' ally to, the Entente Powers in the First World War meant that mass quantities of exogenously sourced money—most of it debt and reparations payments in gold—flowed into the U.S. over the course of the 1920s.

A central bank in thrall to the crude Strong-Form RBD as described above, treating all money as endogenously sourced, non-rehypothecatable credit extended in connection solely with productive projects able to emit new goods and services supplies capable of absorbing all new money, was of course prone to miss the aforementioned developments. The Fed thus failed to act quickly first to 'sterilize' the war debt and reparations influxes of the 1920s, then quickly to counteract, with cash and credit infusions, the credit-crunch that ensued when the property and stock price bubbles inflated by those influxes collapsed at the end of the decade. There lay the cause of the Great Depression, best diagnosed in Irving Fisher's *Booms and Depressions* of 1932.[5]

A proper rendition of the RBD must accordingly be what I'm calling a 'Refined' RBD. It must recognize that most credit-money is indeed endogenously generated and hence requires good allocation toward strictly productive outlets in order to be properly modulated. But it must also recognize the need of exogenous collective action on credit aggregates in response both to (a) 'resale' or rehypothecation activity as described above, and to (b) real exogenous shocks to the money supply, be these inflows or outflows, inflationary or deflationary. This more nuanced and sensitive 'Refined' RBD will accordingly guide the 'restorative reforms' that I lay out below in Part III.

5.3 The Doctrine Refined: Introducing 'Weak-Form' RBD

Reformulating the RBD along more modest, realistic lines is not difficult on light of the theoretical observations laid out in Chapter 4 and the historical lessons drawn out in the foregoing Sections of this Chapter. I'll do that now in the cause of both diagnosing and curing our present central banking, monetary-cum-financial, and hence economic ills in Chapters 6 through 8 below.

Here are the key details, which I will ordinally enumerate with a view to what I hope will be a clear exposition …

First, because our investment markets are decentralized and populated by too many investors for any one person to be able to move them, and because they are stratified into primary, secondary, and tertiary ('derivative') strata, it is often the case that the best that an individual can hope to do is to seek short-term profits by betting on price movements rather than by investing in actual production. This introduces a cleavage between profits and production, while the indefinite extensibility of endogenous credit-money enables the continual widening of that gulf—pursuant to the ReCAP dynamic outlined in Chapter 4. This in turn yields ever-more hollowing out of an economy's productive base and evermore volatile financial and monetary conditions—a fine recent case of which is described in Chapter 8 on current commodity markets below.

Second, the aforementioned facts of our markets mean that no central bank or monetary authority can effectively *modulate* credit-money aggregates without also *allocating* them. This doesn't mean 'picking winners and losers' in any micro-manner. The allocating to which I refer is not allocation between firms or even between industries as such. It is only the most general—and crucial—form of allocation imaginable: that between bona fide productive and merely speculative projects. It is not in general difficult to distinguish between these categories apart from the margin; and at the margin it is easy enough to err on the side of restriction during booms while erring on the side of liberality during busts.

Third, in general, the central bank's allocative task as thus elaborated can be effected by directly or indirectly lending to—that is, by discounting only commercial paper associated with—projects that bid fair to produce more goods, provide more services, or both as will add to the material wealth of the Republic and absorb the very credit-money issued to finance their production or provision. The word 'can' here can, as in effect noted above, be unpacked in terms of necessary conditions, sufficient conditions, or both. As we can glean from the theoretical and historical reflections elaborated above, the discounting of production-associated paper is indeed *necessary* to successful effectuation of the Productive-Republican central bank's allocative function, and hence of its modulatory function as well. But it is no longer *sufficient* to those tasks.

It is to this function that the Fed's regional District Banks are best suited. Hence I will offer a plan for revitalizing Regional Fed Discounting authority and activity such as that done by the 1913 Fed below, in Chapter 7.

Fourth, the Productive-Republican central bank must accordingly supplement its attention to the productive allocation of endogenous credit-money as effectuated through discounting with attention to the stabilizing sterilization or supplementation of exogenously wrought influxes or effluxes of money-flow. Massive purchases of U.S. assets by foreign governments, for example—be they to gain trade advantages by strengthening the dollar or simply to 'park' surpluses in 'safe assets'—or sudden 'capital flight' from American to foreign shores in hopes of 'capitalizing' on 'globalization,' will generally require countercyclical corrective action by the Productive-Republican central bank. This will be necessary in order to assure that the salutary modulatory effects of the central bank's productive endogenous money allocation will not be rendered a nullity by unanticipated or untreated exogenous money 'shocks.'

This function is best handled by the Fed Board (again, 'FRB') and 1935-vintage FOMC, charged with tracking and fine-tuning money aggregates as national wholes. At present, however, the FRB and FOMC are not optimally equipped to discharge this function, for they currently attend only to money market rental—that is, 'interest'—rates, which are but one of what I long ago dubbed the multiple 'Systemically Important Prices and Indices' (again, 'SIPIs') that must be acted upon countercyclically to neutralize exogenous money- and price-shocks economy-wide. Hence I will offer a plan for extending FOMC / New York Fed open market operations (again, 'OMO') to additional systemically important markets below, in Chapter 8.

Finally fifth, also as noted above, even endogenous credit-money extended originally for productive lending can self-amplify, supply-wise, beyond the productive sectors' capacities to produce or provide comprehensively money-absorbing goods and services if rehypothecation risk is not recognized, actively watched out for, and expeditiously counteracted by appropriate discount rate setting—even differentiated such setting supplemented by capital controls when necessary. The greater the typical number of attempted rehypothecations of a given piece of commercial paper, the steeper must grow the discount rate, the ideal being in effect to collapse the sum of the values of all rehypothecations to that of the original bill alone.

This function, like the exogenous money modulation function described above, is likewise best handled by the FRB and 1935-vintage FOMC, charged with tracking and fine-tuning money aggregates as national wholes. And here, moreover, the Fed is in need of no further tools than it already has. All that is requisite is that it understands the nature of the danger described and takes seriously the need both to track and to address it. This is no trivial condition, however, as the Greenspan Fed, in thrall to a coloring book, Ayn Rand-style understanding of our financial markets, failed to see even the most basic preemptively macro-modulatory imperatives of all central banks from about 1987 to 2008. It took years of persistent nagging by the present author and others to make 'macroprudential' financial regulation mainstream again.

That is the full, but I hope not tedious, understanding of what I am calling 'Weak-Form' RBD, which I claim must be the operating system of any central bank or monetary authority meant, like our Fed, to facilitate the financing of continuous, stable and uninterrupted productive development along Productive-Republican lines. Equipped with this understanding, Part III of this book, comprising Chapters 7 and 8 along with a draft bill Appendix, will schematize a 'restoratively reformed' Fed suited to a twenty-first-century Productive Republic. To ease and further motivate the transition, Chapter 6 will elaborate on where are now that the deficiencies of the 1935 Fed are as obvious as those of the 1913 Fed.

Notes

1. What both cases have in common is a single material thing's underlying multiple claims whose aggregate face value exceeds that of the underlying item or event. Note the shared structure between these situations and situations involving over-extending claims against institutions engaging in 'fractional reserve banking.'.
2. See, e.g., Robert Hockett, *Financing the Green New Deal: A Plan of Action and Renewal* (Palgrave 2020).

3. See, of course, Henry Thornton, *An Inquiry into the Nature and Effects of the Paper Currency of Great Britain* (Augustus Kelly 1962 [1845]).
4. See, of course, Thornton, idem.; and Knut Wicksell, Geldzins und Güterpreis (1898).
5. Irving Fisher, *Booms and Depressions* (Macmillan 1932).

CHAPTER 6

The Fed After 1935: Where We Are Now

Abstract This Chapter takes our story up to the present. It shows how the 1935 reforms proved both well- and ill-advised much as the 1913 design of the Fed had proved well- and ill-advised 'from the other direction.' We find that the post-1935 inattention to money endogeneity and the associated imperative of productive allocation ultimately doomed the 1935 project of more effective *money modulation itself*. And that is for reasons rooted in money endogeneity as laid out in Chapter 4. What we missed in 1935 and after was easy to miss for the first several decades following the 1935 reforms, this Chapter shows, thanks to the presence of other laws and institutions, put in place during roughly the same New Deal period, that effectively substituted for the pre-1935 allocative Fed. Chief among these were (a) the New Deal and WWII era Reconstruction Finance Corporation ('RFC'), the most massive allocation-attentive special-purpose development bank in history; (b) tight restrictions on interstate banking and branching established or reinforced in the mid-1940s, which kept banking local hence not Wall Street focused; and (c) the Glass-Steagall separation of banking from speculative, as distinguished from productive, investment activity more generally in 1933. But as the RFC wound down and disbanded in the 1950s, and as Glass-Steagall separations and bank branching restrictions gave way in the 1980s and 1990s, the consequences of a no-longer allocative Fed grew no longer manageable or concealable. One of these consequences is an ever-more hollowed-out productive core of the American economy as Wall Street

R. C. Hockett, *Spread the Fed*,
https://doi.org/10.1007/978-3-031-72051-2_6

financial institutions seek profits in speculating and 'outsourcing' American production to cheap-labor jurisdictions. Another is the decline in real wages and hence struggling middle class that have been hallmarks of our nation's past several decades. *This* has in turn led to increasing reliance by the American middle class on new forms of consumer, mortgage, 'junk,' and student debt, which in turn have fueled multiple bubbles and busts that bring ever more Fed QE rounds that leave the underlying problem of productive hollowing unaddressed while sowing the seeds for repeated and ever worsening asset and consumer price hyperinflations. Additional follow-on dysfunctions have of course been worsening inequality and social division, followed by political breakdown. The only way to 'get our country back,' the Chapter concludes, is to 'get our *Fed* back.' It's to restore our once-great productive and industrially diversified economy, localized development banking, and the healthy middle class that those Productive-Republican institutions and practices historically enabled.

Keywords Banks · Bank-Branching · Bank Holding Company Act · Central Banking · Bubbles · Busts · Collective Action Problems · Consumer Credit · Discounting · Dodd-Frank Act · Endogenous Money · Exogenous Money · Federal Reserve System · Federal Open Market Committee · Financial Holding Companies · Financial Services Modernization Act · Financialization · FOMC · Glass-Steagall Act · Inequality · Monetary Policy · Necessary Conditions · Panics · Productive-Republicanism · Productivist Central Banking · Real Bills Doctrine · Reconstruction Finance Corporation · Recursive Collective Action Problems · Speculation · Sufficient Conditions · Warburg · Wicksell · Strong RBD · Weak RBD

The more detailed early Fed history and reformulated 'Weak' or 'Refined' RBD laid out in Chapter 5 enable us to see now more clearly both why things changed as they did with the banking reforms of 1935 and after, and what the strengths and weaknesses of those reforms were. The *strengths* stemmed from the *greater seriousness* with which the *modulatory* task, and hence exogenous rate-affecting and liquidity-providing action, would now be taken. The *weaknesses* stemmed from the *loss* of attention to the *still*-crucial *allocative* central banking task rooted in most credit-money's continued endogeneity. That's what this Chapter now shows on the way to the full restorative reform plans of Chapters 7 and 8.

6.1 The New Fed of 1935 and After

First, then, how did the errors recounted in Chapter 5, stemming as they did from the erroneous Strong Form or Crude RBD, lead to our radically and unsustainably separating modulation and allocation, monetary and fiscal policy, Fed and Treasury functions? Well, in a word as suggested above, we over-reacted. We effectively decided that, since productive allocation did *not* of itself handle the *whole* of necessary modulation, we would henceforth attend *solely* to modulation as if this were possible *independently* of allocation. *This was precisely half-right*. The upshot was the Banking Act of 1935.

Under the influence of Fisher's not-unsound but nevertheless incomplete rendition of the Quantity Theory of Money (QTM), the Banking Act focused almost exclusively on exogenous money modulation, now conceived technocratically as Fisher, the de facto founder of mathematical economic analysis in the U.S., had himself done. The Act accordingly established an 'independent' Federal Open Market Committee (FOMC) in DC as a new instrument of Fed monetary policy formulation and execution (good), while sidelining the regional Federal Reserve District Banks and their Discounting role (bad). It switched out, in other words, one blade of the scissors for the other.

This of course opened the door to massively destabilizing misallocations of endogenous credit-money. That was muted for a time partly by longstanding Glass-Steagall restrictions on speculative bank lending—bank lending of excess money to stock market speculators in the 1920s having been a primary cause of the bubble and bust of the era. It was also muted by local-focus-ensuring restrictions on interstate banking and branching; by Fed Chairs who well understood, unlike their successors during the Greenspan era, their modulatory roles; and by a very actively allocating *fiscal state* operating through many institutions, especially the Reconstruction Finance Corporation (RFC) and its progeny—FHA, Fannie Mae, SBA prominent among them—up to the 1990s.

But when all of this fell away beginning in the late Carter and Reagan eras, we fell into continual private misallocation of endogenous public credit-money and consequent poor allocation of money aggregates.

Multiple life-, wealth-, and polity-destructive crises have been the upshot. Let us turn briefly now to what happened from the later twentieth century on down to the present, which is far easier to understand in light of the foregoing than it might otherwise have been.

6.2 Compensating Institutions, Their Demise, and Our Trouble Since

For a time the impossibility of indefinitely succeeding at central bank modulation while eschewing central bank allocation was masked by a number of allocative institutional compensations whose modulatory significance was overlooked, presumably owing to the same inattention I am hoping with this Book to rectify.

From the early 1930s through the late 1940s, to begin with, as hinted at above, the explicitly allocative RFC maintained offices in all of the regional Federal Reserve District Banks. This made effectively for something a bit like the pre-1935 'Spread Fed' that the Banking Act of that year ended. From 1933 till the end of the 1940s, this geographically Fed-spread RFC functioned as by far the largest financial institution in the world. Its balance sheet dwarfed those of the post-1929 Wall Street banks combined, including as it did projects as small as Watts barber shops, as large as southeastern U.S. rural electrification programs, and every conceivable size in between. It also financed the entire Second World War mobilization and war production efforts during its final decade—themselves spread all over the nation, with literally every Congressional District hosting war mass-production work.

After the RFC was wound-down near the end of the 1940s, in turn, banking and thrift regulation, much of it sponsored by Fed-founder Carter Glass, continued to perform a critical modulation-assisting credit-allocative function until the end of the twentieth century. Regulation Q, for example, enabled mortgage-financing thrifts to attract more deposit moneys than would otherwise have been possible, thereby directing more credit to home purchase by America's growing post-WWII middle class.

Restrictions on interstate banking and branching, for their parts, kept commercial banks local till 1997, which in turn kept bank-generated credit flowing to smaller, more locally focused businesses across the nation rather than simply toward Wall Street and Wacker Drive stock and commodity speculators. And of course other federal institutions of home-, small business, and agricultural finance—by far most of them, including the Small Business Administration ('SBA'), the Federal Housing Administration ('FHA') and the Federal National Mortgage Association ('FNMA'), former subsidiaries of the RFC—functioned as continuing federal work toward modulation-assisting credit allocation.

Complementing these compensating institutions were labor law and tax reformed which had the effect of channeling more money toward goods-buying hence production-encouraging working people and less toward financial market-playing *rentiers*.

The upshot of all of these pragmatic policy measures was a thirty-year, largely bubble- and bust-free postwar macroeconomic boom that effectively made the modern American middle class—the 'Great Moderation.' Even as the population rapidly grew, rates of home-ownership, diploma-earning, and per capita income rose steadily. Wage and income rises matched national productivity gains year after year, and inflation was kept under wraps by a tax code whose capital gains and top marginal income rates were the highest in all of American history. Here was a case, then, in which the proverbial 'rising tide' did 'lift all boats.' It was the moderation—the volatility-suppression—of that 'Great Moderation' itself that made this possible. And it was the income equalization, credit allocation, money modulation, and utility-style regulation that underwrote that equilibrium.

So what happened? What took us from the so-called 'Great Moderation' of 1945–75 to 2008 and today? The answer lies in a number of mutually reinforcing developments that combined to restore the immoderate economy of the 1920s to postwar America. The seeds of the trouble were sown by the Vietnam war spending of the Johnson years, which when added to Great Society spending brought both monetary inflation and social unrest. The latter developments ultimately brought reactionaries like Richard Nixon, Jimmy Carter, and Ronald Reagan to political power—Presidents whose attitudes toward the essential role of taxation and public institutions in 'private' economic arrangements differed markedly from those of their predecessors from Roosevelt through Johnson.

These administrations and, even more, the administrations and Congresses that followed steadily undid what the New Deal and Great Society had done, in effect if not intention, to keep in place early Fed style allocation that enabled effective money modulation. Labor legislation and its enforcement were weakened, and organized labor came both to be viewed as and to be treated as a 'public enemy.' Cross-border trade liberalization further weakened worker bargaining power. The tax code became steadily less progressive and public spending on public goods—notably critical infrastructure and education—was curtailed.

All the while, deregulation of what Orwellianly began to be called 'the financial services industry' simultaneously reintroduced '20s style risk to the macro-economy while presenting policymakers with a temporarily attractive alternative to redistributive labor and tax policy—cheap credit in place of real incomes to maintain growth-fueling consumer demand. Repeal of Glass-Steagall and prohibition of derivatives regulation, respectively, by the Financial Services Modernization Act of 1999 and the Commodity Futures Modernization Act of 2000, completed the process of enabling credit-flows to run massively toward speculative betting on price movements in secondary financial and tertiary derivatives markets in the northeast, not productive manufacturing and services firms in our continent-spanning republic's interior.

In essence, the nation moved from a regime of public provisioning of public goods and public encouragement of shared gains from growth, to a regime of publicly encouraged financial 'innovation' geared toward new forms of consumer and mortgage borrowing, by the great bulk of working Americans, from the small class of wealthy Americans and massive financial institutions. The result was an explosion of volatile mortgage debt, consumer debt, and education debt unparalleled since the 1920s. And so, predictably, massive asset price bubble, asset price bust, and debt-deflationary aftermath struck once again in the late 1990s and early 2000s era of the Greenspan Fed as had occurred eighty years earlier at the end of the early Fed period.

And so we had more and more to use deliberately speculation-encouraging, bubble-inflating modulatory tools—including QE post-2008 and *further* bubble-inflating innovations since 2020—to prevent macroeconomic collapse in the face of now decades-long, poor-allocation-associated productive decline. For the same recursive collective action predicaments described above in connection with bubbles and busts have led individual investors rationally to seek immediate profits in secondary and tertiary market bets rather than long-term wealth creation through 'patient capital' investment in our productive sectors.

Absent concerted collective agency in the name of productive capital allocation, these ongoing collective action predicaments—a 'deep structural' condition of all disaggregated market exchange when it is how things are arranged even on the capital supply side, not just the product demand side, of our macroeconomy—will continue to hollow us out. The 'endgame' is terminal decline toward terminal collapse. Unless, that is, we can recombine concerted public credit-allocative action with concerted public credit-modulatory action as we used to do so well.

Must we continue this way? Is it just crises henceforth, followed by temporary fiscal-monetary coordinations, followed by ever-worse crises?

Not at all. The key is to recover what was right in the Real Bills Doctrine as described in the Refined formulation developed above, while leaving what was wrong on the ash heap. The key is, in other words, to restore the pre-1935 blade of the scissors *while* keeping the post-1935 blade of the scissors.

PART III

From National Degeneration to Regenerative Fed Decentralization

The political emergence, midway through the present century's second decade, of a bottomlessly petulant, ceaselessly tantrum-prone, obsessively 'rage-tweeting' old man personifying lumpish fear and resentment is instructively interpretable, I believe, as a clue to something important about our post-1935 Fed in a post-New Deal world. It is a clue to what was lost in 1935, what remained unreclaimed after 2008, and to what is in store for our nation and central bank soon if we do not reverse the trajectory that produced this man.[1]

What remains unreclaimed is what this Book aims to reclaim – the best of the pre-1935 Fed with best of the post-1935. That is sound allocation and therefore sound modulation. Chapters 7 and 8 now accordingly show how to do this. They show how to re-spread our Fed. Chapter 7 shows how to do so across regions. Chapter 8 shows how to do so across markets. Between the two of them, they yield a Fed as congenial to Carter Glass and Paul Warburg as to Irving Fisher and Milton Friedman, to Hamilton and Lincoln as to Jefferson and Reagan, and to Thornton and Wicksell as to Smith and Walras.

[1] Id.

CHAPTER 7

Crises and De- or Re-Generation

Abstract This Chapter begins the task of designing a fully updated 1913-style Fed, with retained 1935-style characteristics, along lines suggested by the historical and theoretical work of the prior chapters. This task is greatly aided both by the fact that 'we've done this before,' and by the fact that we even began an incipient update like that I design here during the Covid pandemic, in the forms of the Municipal Liquidity Facility ('MLF') and the Main Street Lending ('MSL') programs introduced in 2020. While flawed in their execution owing to our having vested responsibility for them in only two Federal Reserve District Banks—the New York and Boston Feds—in conception these plans were promising, as countless white papers, opinion pieces, and Fed and municipal advisory calls that I put out over 2020–21 made clear. There is no reason, the Chapter accordingly argues, that we can't get those things right now. The 'Spread Fed' plan that I accordingly blueprint in this Chapter also updates the 1913 distribution of Fed District Banks in a manner that reflects changes our regional economies have undergone over the past century.

Keywords Banks · Central Banking · Bubbles · Busts · Collective Action Problems · Covid · Credit · Discounting · Dollar · Elastic Currency · Endogenous Money · Exogenous Money · Federal Reserve System · Federal Open Market Committee · Fisher · FOMC · Glass · Great Depression · Monetary Policy · Main Street Lending Programs · MLF · MSLP · Municipal Liquidity Facility · Necessary Conditions · Pandemic ·

R. C. Hockett, *Spread the Fed*,
https://doi.org/10.1007/978-3-031-72051-2_7

Panics · Productivism · Productivist Central Banking · Real Bills Doctrine · Recursive Collective Action Problems · Smith · Speculation · Steuart · Sufficient Conditions · Walras · Warburg · Wicksell · Strong RBD · Weak RBD

Though it seems to have been widely forgotten, the post-crash 1930s raised the specter not only of fascist and communist revolution in the U.S., but also of federal disintegration akin both to that of the Civil War era and to that underway now.[1] Californians sought to bar 'Okie' migration to their state after the Dust Bowl calamity.[2] Southerners resisted northern pressure to stop disenfranchising non-white and non-male citizens in an era where who governed determined who ate and who didn't.[3]

Regions of the country where finance, manufacturing, or agriculture predominated argued bitterly over trade and monetary policy, in the face of a shrinking global economy in which liberal trade imperiled some while retrenchment imperiled others.[4] Regions of the country with largely German-, Irish-, English-, or Italian-descended populations in turn squabbled over whom if anyone to support in a gathering European cold war.[5] And so on.

One way to think of the New Deal is accordingly not only as the bare minimum that was necessary to preserve both 'capitalism' and some semblance of political *democracy* in the U.S., as is routinely remarked, but also as the minimum necessary to preserve our federal union itself. The sole way to avert terminal entropy in the face of a rapidly shrinking 'pie' was first to make sure all could eat, and then to resume growing the 'pie.'

And this is what Roosevelt *did*. From the banking and monetary reforms rehearsed above, through massive public works projects and investment done by a Reconstruction Finance Corporation patterned after the War Finance Corporation mentioned above, to early renditions of the later Vista, CORE, and AmeriCorps programs that brought young people to new parts of the country to aid redevelopment, the New Deal fashioned a new and endurable, hence durable, America. We returned to being an America in which material opportunity again waxed as resentment and separatist tendencies waned.

The twenty-first-century Fed after 2008, unlike the twentieth-century Fed after 1929, did remarkable work to preserve and protect our monetary and financial systems during the Great Recession. But nothing on the scale of the New Deal ever crystalized to rectify the underlying dysfunctions of our 'real' economy, which had brought on the 1929 and 2008 crashes in the first place.[6] Loans weren't forgiven, wages weren't raised, and virtually nothing was built.[7] In consequence, incomes and wealth accumulation below the top of the national distributions continued to lag even as publicly rescued *rentier*-owned businesses grew ever better at reconstituting employees as 'gig' workers who didn't enjoy labor protections, living wages, health insurance, or retirement insurance.[8]

The 'precariat' that accordingly grew into an ever-larger part of our population accordingly seethed, and sought succor in political visions that could both explain their plights and offer means of redress.[9] As in the post-1929 era, so now the movements that emerged from this cauldron took left and right forms. The first vested its hopes in avowed 'Democratic Socialist' (in fact, more New Dealer[10]) Bernie Sanders. The second opted for the more Mussolini-reminiscent Trump. Like in Europe during the 1930s, so here in the 2010s the more fascistic element, trading on cultural symbols of a cherished national past, at least temporarily won the day. In this case, however, they brought a wrinkle not seen earlier in Europe…

In contrast to the European fascism of the 1930s, which consolidated national at the expense of regional and local authority, the American fascism of the 2010s worked in the other direction. It exploited class and ethnic divisions in ways that divided the nation regionally, and in so doing undermined those regions' last vestige of nationally shared agency—our federal government. This form of fascism's architects, perhaps best personified by Bannon if not Trump himself, professed *devolution* as their '*revolution*.'[11]

The Bannonites' professed purpose was to 'deconstruct' the Progressive and New Deal eras' administrative state, and to leave ever more federal functions to, if to anything, sub-federal units of government.[12] States and cities would be our sites of collective agency, or there would be none such at all. It is easy to formulate both cultural and political-economic explanations for this inverted form of fascism in the U.S. Culturally speaking, fascism's nostalgia for a nation's past in America for obvious reasons looked back, not to 'the glory that was Rome' or Prussia—two consolidated polities—as did Italian and German fascism, but to the 'greatness' that was pre- Civil War, not-yet-fully-integrated *nineteenth-century* America.[13] Andrew Jackson, not Caesar, was *our* Caesar.[14]

State and local government also tended in large part to be more ethnically and culturally homogeneous than the federal government could be. That would presumably have exercised an attraction to ethno-fascists in a multiethnic polity like the U.S. even when less pronounced in less ethnically heterogeneous 'national' polities elsewhere in the world. Where political economy is concerned, meanwhile, the wealthy interests that funded the likes of Bannon, Trump, and their cronies seem to have preferred state and local over federal governance because smaller state and local governments were more consistently 'capturable' than was the federal government.[15]

The upshot with which we've been living ever since is now plain to see. Federal agencies were hollowed out as the Trump administration fomented shrinkage through attrition both by routinely firing officials on trifling pretexts and by not filling the consequent or even prior vacancies.[16] When it appointed people at all, moreover, it appointed personal cronies and loyal toadies devoid of either competence or experience in agencies' mandate-fields.[17] This development of course didn't go unnoticed over the years,[18] but its consequences have proved quite dramatic during the COVID pandemic. Its sequel, were Trump and his 'Project 2025' to succeed in the 2024 election, would be even more so.

The Trump administration's unwillingness to mobilize any national productive or mitigation response to the pandemic of 2020–22 that might compare to the earlier Wilson and Roosevelt administrations' responses to the First and Second World Wars was widely remarked.[19] Also widely discussed was a dawning awareness that cities, states, and compacts of states are in some cases all we have left where collective address of such collective action challenges as the pandemic is concerned.[20] In effect, we devolved back to a state of our union in which states and their subdivisions were our sole means of concerted national action. It was as if we were once again living under the Articles of Confederation, or perhaps in the Confederate States of America. *They*—our states and cities—were for a while our new 'administrative state,' at least till we once again got a national executive that believes in the national project as we did in late 2020.[21]

It was against this backdrop—and as a *response* to the devolution just noted—that the Fed's Community QE and Main Street QE initiatives of 2020 were best understood. The mentioned backdrop did more than explain the emergence of the new facilities, however. It also hinted at what we still have to do if we wish in the future to optimize such programs—that is, in my parlance, to re-spread the Fed. As noted above, this includes far more extensive '(re-)distribution' of the Federal Reserve System even than Community QE and Main Street QE occasioned. This Chapter accordingly shows how to build out from those initiatives, which I'll view as incipient efforts at once again spreading the Fed, and thereby making our Fed once again what it was always meant to be.

7.1 Once More Unto the Breach: Community & Main Street QE as Substitute Federal Administration

Let's start with a brief bit of background on Community and Main Street QE themselves, the temporary Covid-era innovations that reprised what Fed once had been and showed what going forward it can be …

In late March of 2020, Congress passed the Coronavirus Aid, Relief, and Economic Security ('CARES') Act.[22] Among the Acts many provisions and measures were new appropriations for Treasury to use in initially capitalizing new Fed lending facilities. These in effect rendered Treasury the equity holder, the Fed the levering bank in something akin to a 'family' of investment funds.

Several weeks after the CARES Act's passage, the Fed Board of Governors announced plans to open a new 'Municipal Liquidity Facility' to assist U.S. States and Localities suffering acute liquidity shortages while working to address the COVID-19 pandemic.[23] Several considerations were said to have prompted the move. Prominent among them were three mutually reinforcing developments that had intensified in then-recent weeks.

First, States and Cities were facing spikes in required expenditure as they took on the role of front-line responders to the pandemic and its consequences.[24] Second and simultaneously, States' and Cities' principal sources of revenue—in particular, sales taxes, income taxes, and property taxes—had dramatically contracted as businesses suspended operations and taxpayers 'sheltered in place.' And third, the $4 trillion municipal bond market, the health of which is critical not only for States and their Subdivisions, but also for other securities markets, had experienced unprecedented volatility since February.

Against the backdrop of these developments, public health officials, State and Local officials, and bond market professionals had called since early March for Fed intervention in the markets for State and Municipal securities ('munis') to stabilize prices, restore confidence to muni-investors, and ease the liquidity strains already hampering State and City pandemic response efforts. With passage of the Coronavirus Aid, Relief, and Economic Security ('CARES') Act by Congress less than two weeks earlier on March 2, it had become clear that both our federal legislature and our Fed and Treasury would be heeding those calls.[25]

The Fed and Treasury's means of heeding of this particular call was the MLF. The Facility operated under the auspices of Section 13(3) of the Federal Reserve Act ('FRA'), which grants the Federal Reserve emergency lending authority in exigent circumstances.[26] The Fed exercises this authority through purchase and hence 'monetization' of short-term debt instruments—a practice known in finance parlance as 'discounting,' the very same practice recounted above in Parts I and II in connection with early Fed history.

In effect, the Fed would temporarily swap its own dollar liabilities, which are legal tender, for liabilities of its counterparties, which were not legal tender. A counterparty would thereby be rendered 'liquid'—possessed of sufficient cash to spend on what ever it had to spend to work past whatever difficulties it might have been facing—until its debt instruments reached maturity. At that point the instruments would be either redeemed in full or, were the option available, 'rolled-over.'

Needless to say, the Fed made abundant use of the Section 13(3) authority to afford liquidity assistance to many financial institutions and markets during the crash of 2008 and the post-2008 Great Recession, and thus gained considerable experience with this funding mechanism even in the present century. It was accordingly not the use of 13(3) that is new in 2020, but the use of the facility to aid States and their political Subdivisions. That had indeed been unprecedented in the modern era.

The new MLF, like its predecessor facilities after 2008, operated through a newly formed special purpose vehicle (SPV)—in essence, a legal trustable to purchase, hold, and sell financial assets. In this case the assets in question were State and Municipal paper, then called 'Eligible Notes' in the MLF Term Sheet, whose salient characteristics I will turn to below.[27]

The MLF SPV was initially capitalized with $35 billion from the U.S. Treasury, Congressionally appropriated for the purpose by the aforementioned CARES Act. On this basis, the Fed would itself lend $500 billion, rendering Treasury the equity investor and hence first risk-bearer in the SPV while the Fed served as leverage-provider. While the structure just described has, as noted before, been a familiar one since the 2008 crisis, the 'substance' of its new 2020 operations was quite new and noteworthy—indeed unprecedented and 'game-changing'—in ways that were critically important for States and their Subdivisions faced with pandemic-caused hardship. At least three features bear special mention in this connection, all having to do with 'eligibility' as defined by the Term Sheet.

The Term Sheet defined *Eligible Notes* as 'tax anticipation notes (TANs), tax and revenue anticipation notes (TRANs), bond anticipation notes (BANs), [or] other similar short-term notes issued by Eligible Issuers.'[28] Intriguingly, it ultimately permitted notes of up to three years' maturity, after having initially surprised observers already with allowance for notes of up to two years' maturity in early April.[29]

Both moves were surprising because the Term Sheets' references to revenue-anticipation instrument clearly were meant to underscore perceptions, brought by the MLF's very name, that the Facility was nothing more than a tide-over liquidity support mechanism. Three-year notes enable far more to be characterized as 'revenue-anticipating' in character than anything ordinarily thought meant for 'liquidity.' This was but one surprising, and indeed welcome, feature of the MLF—particularly for those, like myself in this book, eager to restore pre-1935 Fed discounting practices.

Eligible Issuers under the MLF authority were defined with surprising breadth, as were Eligible Notes.[30] The Term Sheet stipulated that they would comprise all U.S. States and the District of Columbia, U.S. Counties with populations exceeding 500,000, and U.S. Cities with populations exceeding 250,000.[31] The Term Sheet also permitted 'States [to] request that the SPV purchase Eligible Notes *in excess* of the applicable limit in order to assist political subdivisions and instrumentalities that [were] not eligible for the Facility,' and also expressly provided for Multi-State Entities established by interstate compacting among any two or more States.[32]

Finally, 'Eligible Use' of Fed funds gained through sale of 'Eligible Notes' tracked the criteria that defined those Notes themselves. The Term Sheet stipulated that proceeds of Note sales were intended to be used 'to help manage the cash flow impact of [a] income tax deferrals resulting from an extension of an income tax filing deadline; [b] potential reductions of tax and other revenues or increases in expenses related to or resulting from the COVID-19 pandemic; and [c] requirements for the payment of principal and interest on obligations.'[33]

The Fed sought in these words to encourage perception of the MLF as a tide-over facility meant to assist counterparties in, as the Term Sheet put it, 'managing [their] cash flows.'[34] Crucially, however, as noted above, 36-month paper is no ordinary 'liquidity' instrument, and other sections of the Term Sheet emphasized the prospect of longer-term 'rollover' of Note debt, while analysts, myself included, for many months anticipated expansion of coverage from 36-month to 60-month paper. Moreover, as noted above, three-year loans already allow for far more uses to be characterized as 'revenue-anticipation' measures than those customarily associated with that phrase. Five-year loans would of course have allowed for many more.

The Fed's encouraging perceptions of the MLF as a short-term liquidity support mechanism on the one hand, while providing assistance that was in substance far longer-term on the other hand, is probably attributable to two considerations. The first is that the Fed hoped to avoid provoking longtime Fed-skeptics with peculiarly early nineteenth-century worldviews into fulminating against central bank 'overreach' and calling yet again to 'end the Fed.'[35] The second is that the delicate task of all central banks is to afford confidence that they will do 'whatever it takes' to prevent worsening on the part of a crisis on the one hand, without stoking panic by appearing *already to be taking* the most extraordinary measures that it might 'take' on the other hand.[36]

This is why Fed Chairs and indeed all central bankers throughout history have engaged in that characteristic 'double-talk' which observers regularly mock and satirize.[37] It is also why I urged at the time that States and their Subdivisions, along with any Compacts they might have formed to make further use of the MLF, should not be daunted by any terminology connoting mere 'liquidity' or 'short-term tide-over' that they encountered in the Term Sheet or heard from officials. The window dressing is one thing, that which is passed through the window another.[38]

I accordingly advised a then ever-growing number of Cities, States, and prospective Compacts of States to look at the substance of what Term Sheet *terms* actually *authorize* rather than taking at face value what the *terminology* used in the Term Sheet or by officials in their official pronouncements might customarily *connote*. I told them that they should assume that the Fed would indeed do 'whatever it takes,' including through further easing of Term Sheet terms, to prevent States and Cities from collapsing under the pressures brought on by the pandemic.[39] And, I continued, they should have unrelentingly pushed for the further easing just mentioned, in the interest of actually ***doing*** 'whatever it takes' to arrest and reverse both the pandemic and its economic and social fallout.[40]

In addition to the breadth with which Eligible Notes, Eligible Issuers, and Eligible Uses were defined, there were several further indicators that suggested the MLF would become a critically important part of state and municipal finance were the pandemic to continue. One was the Fed's having postponed the closing of the window by months even before the Facility had gone operational—from the end of September 2020, as planned in early April, to the end of the year, as announced at the end of April. Another indicator appeared in the Fed's own interpretive announcements …[41]

Chairman Powell and the Board publicly encouraged a very 'flexible' *interpretation* of all conditional *language* found in the Term Sheet.[42] They also repeatedly stated that they would be monitoring the municipal debt ('muni') markets for signs of resumed volatility, with an eye to intervening yet further to stabilize them if and as necessary.[43] Combined with the Term Sheet terms themselves as described above, and with the many openings for extension and exception specified in the Term Sheet, these amounted to assurances that the MLF was a 'work in progress' whose scope could in theory expand if and as the need for it expanded.[44]

The Fed's new *Main Street* QE facilities, which were if anything more promising even than its *Community* QE facility just described, afforded further encouragement on this score …

The story of the Main Street QE facilities, one of which was announced the same day as the MLF—viz., the PPPLF, on April 9th of 2020– and the others of which were announced at the end of April, was much like that of the Community QE facility. There were just a few added wrinkles stemming from the facts that (a) there were several of the former, and (b) 'small business' is legally a more amorphous category than is 'State' or 'State Subdivision' in our constitutional order.

The idea behind all of them was to assist smaller firms that lacked traditional credit ratings and, relatedly, ready access to capital markets. They comprised a 'Main Street New Loan Facility' (MSNLF), a 'Main Street

Expanded Loan Facility' (MSELF), a 'Main Street Primary Loan Facility' (MPLF), and a 'Payroll Protection Program Loan Facility' (PPPLF).

The latter—the PPPLF—probably received most attention. It was also the most like the MLF inasmuch as the Fed took no overt credit risk through it, while in the case of the first three, it overtly lent.

Because small firms tend to be short on in-house legal assistance and accounting savvy, the Fed announced upon starting these facilities that it would employ private sector banking institutions to originate and service most Main Street QE loans. Banks would have to retain 5% of all loans on their balance sheets in the case of the first two facilities, 15% in the case of the third. As with the MLF, Treasury also took an equity stake, employing $75 billion from its CARES Act appropriation to absorb any losses the facilities might incur beyond the bank stakes.

In the case of the PPPLF, as noted, the Fed assumed no overt credit risk. The Small Business Administration (SBA), as noted earlier a former subsidiary of the aforementioned RFC, was to guarantee the loans, which would function as conditional grants. Banks would originate them like other Main Street QE loans. Thereafter the Fed would purchase the loans from the banks, monetizing them much as it would monetize State and Municipal debt through the MLF. This would of course free up money for banks to lend more—rather as adding public banks to Community QE, as discussed further below, could have levered up MLF money.

Banks would continue to service loans even after moving them from their balance sheets to the Fed's balance sheet.[45] Eligible Businesses under Main Street QE were those with up to 15,000 employees or $5 billion in 2019 annual revenues.[46] Borrowing firms also had to maintain and certify compliance with sundry regulatory restrictions, including limitations on executive compensation, stock buybacks, and dividend payments. Like States and Cities under Community QE, they had also to attest to requiring assistance for *pandemic*-related reasons.[47]

It would be difficult to read the Community QE and Main Street QE Term Sheets and the sundry statements made by the Fed around them without concluding that the Fed had been eyeing the federal non-response to our national pandemic and drawn at least one tentative bipartite policy conclusion.[48] The first conclusion was that our states and cities had, as I put it above, become in effect our new federal agencies, and had accordingly to be *funded* as federal agencies.[49] The second was that our small businesses were significant sites of combined productive importance, employment vulnerability, and inadequate market funding.

If this read was correct, than we could have anticipated, as I did at the time, even more expansion in future—including extension of the facilities just elaborated to Tribes and Territories as Congress enjoined, and extending eligible maturities on State and Municipal debt to five or more years as bond market analysts and the 'smart money' in muni markets already anticipated.[50] But as I argued at the time, we should not just *anticipate* more if this read on Community and Main Street QE were plausible. We should also have *expected* it, in the 'demand' sense of 'expect.' And I now argue that we must push now, post-pandemic, for a *yet more fulsome* re-regionalization of the Fed. We turn now to that project.[51]

7.2 A (Re-) Distributed Fed

The Covid pandemic highlighted not only the rot that had been underway both on and under the surface of our federal administration since 2017, but also the lingering differences between our many local and regional economies that either were re-implicated by the crisis itself. New York City's Covid pandemic was very different from Bismarck, North Dakota's Covid pandemic. And both of those Covid pandemics were very different from Atlanta's and Ithaca's Covid pandemics.

These differences were not, of course, differences in the genetic structure of the Coronavirus as manifest in different geographic locations. They were differences in impact, rooted in differences among local practices, local policy orientations and policy measures, local cultures, population densities, primary industries, and other determinants of what boil down to differing local and regional economies and consequent local and regional needs during times of distress.

In this sense, the national economy in 2020 wasn't altogether unlike what it had been in 1913. It was, and is, still subject to significant regional variation along newly or once again salient dimensions. And as elaborated above in Parts I and II, the federated structure of our Federal Reserve 'System' was designed in part precisely to allow for differing monetary *responses* to such differing conditions.

What will it be, then, to restore at least in part that once significant latitude for variation among Regional Fed Banks? What will it be, relatedly, to 'thicken' the nexus of communication between each Regional Fed District Bank and its constituent states and communities again? What might—or ought—a re-federated or re-distributed Fed look like?

I think that it means at least three things. First is to reopen and indeed formalize regular channels of communication and joint planning between Regional Fed Banks on the one hand, and state and city finance and economic development personnel on the other hand. This we should do, I argued in 2020 and still maintain now, both over the duration of the new Community and Main Street QE facilities and beyond. We can think of these lines of communication and joint planning as 'synapses' enabling joint deliberation and action on the part of our distributed central bank and our continentally distributed citizens' primary day-to-day agents—their state and city governments.

Next is to distribute the actual *administration* both of Community and Main Street QE and of all other relevant Section 13 Fed Facilities, in 2020 and in future, over *all* of the Regional Feds rather than housing them all in the New York Fed. The latter was a practice that, whatever sense it might have made for Fed Facilities that benefit only Wall Street banks like those of 2008 and after, is as unjust to both FRBNY personnel and our continentally distributed citizenry as it is inefficient and pragmatically untenable in the case of Facilities that are *not* meant solely to assist Wall Street. We can think of this as a kind of revitalized 'nervous system' and 'musculature,' restored to use after decades of atrophy, which will enable our central bank again to partner with decentered cities, states, community banks, and small businesses to make local and regional development actually *happen*.

Also second is to revisit the current regional distribution of Regional Fed Banks itself in light of the many changes to our national economy's regional structure that have occurred since 1913. It is, to say the least, idiosyncratic to have only one Federal Reserve Bank for California and the entire American West while having two Federal Reserve Banks in Missouri and eight to its east. We can think of this as a kind of 'musculoskeletal rebalancing,' pursuant to which one breaks the habit of overusing some muscles too much and others too little, and thereby brings his or her spine back into proper alignment in a manner that clears many fundamental dysfunctions associated with *improper* alignment.

And third is to re-distribute the Fed not only across regions, but also across markets. That is, rather than focusing only on money markets, the Fed's modulatory actions must attend to all markets in what I have long ago dubbed 'Systemically Important Prices and Indices'—or 'SIPIs' for short. I'll address these matters in turn—the first two in this Chapter, and the third in the next Chapter.

7.3 Fed, State, and Municipal 'Synapses': Continuous Communication & Planning

The first move toward 're-distribution' that I have in mind is quite humble, which is the sole reason I was able in 2020 to do anything about it from my end as a former Fed lawyer. It is for all Regional Feds to initiate regular 'town hall' sessions and 'speed dial' access for relevant officials in all cities in their regions—at the very least all cities in which the Fed maintains branch offices or runs Section 13 Facilities.

These could begin in 'Zoom Rooms' where necessary for the time being—a modality that not only comports with social distancing as presently required, but also enables participation even by people located in cities where the Fed *lacks* Reserve Banks or branch offices at present. In future, moreover, the Fed should hold these in literally all cities that are themselves eligible, or are the homes of small banks or businesses eligible, to access Section 13 Facilities—from Community QE to Main Street QE and beyond—and open additional branch offices accordingly.

The purpose of these meetings and speed dial access will be at least two-fold. First, they will facilitate two-way information flows and joint planning between the Fed, our cities, and their enterprises concerning Community and Main Street QE needs on the one hand, and these facilities' eligibilities and logistics on the other hand. And second, they will 'break the ice' and set the stage for more fulsome, regular, and permanent Fed/local communication and planning on the other hand—a need apt to grow urgent as new Section 13 Facilities, including for community banks and small business, are developed. In this way they'll make the Fed much more useful an institution to our people, their enterprises, and their cities and states than it is now. It will begin the long march toward becoming a true 'People's Fed.'[52]

As I say, I worked to set this particular process in motion even during the pandemic in 2020.[53] That process was eased somewhat by (a) much past work I did with cities after the 2008 crash in connection with my eminent domain plan for underwater mortgage loans on the one hand, (b) my longstanding involvement in the community and public banking movements, and (c) my previous employment by the New York Fed itself, along with sundry consulting jobs for the Fed and Treasury, on the other hand.[54] But as I also say, this was quite humble work, and was but a humble achievement once achieved.

Merely opening lines of communication for joint planning will not do much good if they do not *remain* open. And for them to remain open they must actually be put to manifestly good *use*. Getting Community and Main Street QE off the ground by assisting with planning possible uses, drawing up actual papers to get Note sales and bespoke lending started, and continuing to advise over the course of fund use would have been one obviously valuable deployment. But there must be many *more* uses in *future* if continuing linkages are to be valuable. And, as it happens, there are.

7.4 Fed, State, and Municipal 'Neuro-Musculature': Distributed Facility Administration

The next thing that needs doing is more difficult than the first but also essential—especially if the 'synapses' just recommended are to have any point other than pleasant dreaming. I refer to the urgent need to end the practice of housing all Section 13 Facilities in one or two Fed District Banks like the New York or Boston Feds, and instead housing them in *all* relevant regional Feds. Any future Community or Main Street QE as operative in Atlanta, for example should be administered by the Atlanta Fed. In Detroit there should be a Detroit branch office of the Chicago Fed, in Hawaii a branch office of the San Francisco Fed, and so on.

These were '*Municipal* Liquidity' and '*Small* Business Lending' Facilities, after all, not Wall Street primary dealer facilities. Why should their work all be done in but one municipality—one tiny island at the far Atlantic extremity of a continent-spanning republic—dominated by global megabanks?

The reasons for a more distributed administration should be obvious. Fed folk on site in locations meant actually to benefit will have much better understandings of needs and of ways to help than will folk thousands of miles, scores of regional economies, and multiple time zones away. They will also be more approachable, and reachable, by affected parties. This is precisely why the Fed maintains personnel permanently on site at regulated banks,[55] and it is why we opted for a federated Fed in the first place, in 1913.[56] And whatever regional differences prompting that federated structure in 1913 might have receded since then are more than replaced now by *new* differential needs, both in the midst of our crisis and beyond. And we should of course welcome this, inasmuch as we always have valued both subsidiarity in governance and a wide distribution of small nimble enterprises and small community lenders.[57]

For the duration of the pandemic, for example, cities like New York and San Francisco, with high population densities, had to find or appropriate hospital space, protective gear, and testing equipment quite quickly. They also, more morbidly, had to find means of safely storing the dead until such time as these remains could be reverently dealt with. These cities also have sizable nursing home, public housing, and homeless populations that implicate specific municipal and associated business needs. They also have extensive and exceedingly vulnerable public transport and livery systems.

Other cities, like Boston and Chicago, have lower population densities but corresponding transportation challenges. And 'majority minority' cities like Atlanta and New Orleans, or financially strapped cities like Detroit and Newark, and rural townships and variegated counties and regions with large populations of non-English speakers, ... these all experience pandemics and other challenges in their own ways too.

To these different public health needs correspond different financing needs, in respect not only of Note or bespoke loan maturities but also of designated uses and preferable term structures. A good deal of advice will be needed, meaning in turn that a good many advisors and a good bit of locally variable differential knowledge and expertise among them will be needed. It is absurd and unjust to FRBNY staffers themselves to suppose that a few of them in lower Manhattan can handle this all even to their own, let alone to their beneficiaries' satisfaction. And I say this as one who has worked among this gifted group and knows them to be among the most brilliant, conscientious, and hard-working corps of public servants in the world.

Similar observations, unsurprisingly, hold of small business lending and pretty much any Fed facility that in 2020 was or one day will be meant to assist parties for whom *regional* differences translate into *needs* differences.[58] Think of how various the needs and concerns of a small tractor repair shop in South Dakota or landscaping service in Florida or bodega in Queens are apt to be, for example, making use of different supply chains operating in different markets in which different payment practices prevail as they do. Again, then, why task a few staffers in lower Manhattan with managing all fund application and fund distribution activity? The *fund* distribution requires more *Fed* distribution if we are to do the thing right.

Again, as discussed above in Parts I and II of this Book, none of these considerations were foreign to the Fed's founders over a century ago. For, also again, such considerations are part of why they 'distributed' the Fed in the way that they did in the first place. What is requisite now is to restore something like that regime—at the very least, for the administration of all Section 13 Facilities meant to aid sectors that are distributed over our full continental republic rather than concentrated on or near Wall Street in lower Manhattan.

But I will go one further, and suggest that it shouldn't be Section 13 emergency facilities alone, but should be all 'real' primary market, as distinguished from speculative secondary and tertiary market, development finance that should be directly facilitated by our Regional Feds. And that will be optimized by not only re-distributing the Fed, but also by gently redistributing (no hyphen) the Regional *Feds*.

7.5 Fed, State, and Municipal 'Muculo-Skeletal Alignment': From Re-Distribution to Redistribution

As noted above in Parts I and II, the Fed's framers envisaged and instituted a *federated* Fed, but they did so in 1913, when the nation's economy was regionally distributed in ways different from now. One Fed Bank in California and two in Missouri, along with others in Atlanta, Richmond, Philadelphia, Cleveland, Minneapolis, and so on, actually made at least some productive, monetary, and political sense back then, before the rust belt had rusted and the Sunshine State had become the Silicon State (in at least two senses), among other things. But it makes no sense save perhaps 'path-dependence' sense now.

For the Fed to grow more intimately and continuously involved in assisting with the financing of continuous productive development as just envisaged, then, it will have to be not only re-distributed, but redistributed. That is to say that its Regional *Banks* will have to re-synch with the regional *economies* that we actually *have*, not merely those we once *had*.

I see two mutually complementary ways to do this without raising hackles or 'stepping on toes.' One is simply to incorporate additional new Federal Reserve Banks, rather than trying to 'reshuffle' those that we have. Think of it as a central banking counterpart to 'Court packing' that doesn't do mischief, but instead simply adds sorely needed functionality. So, say, Missouri keeps its two Feds, but California now gets one in Los Angeles in addition to that in San Francisco—Southern and Northern California being so different, after all, in their economies, their cultures, and (thank Heaven) their tastes. Cleveland and Philadelphia, too, keep their Feds, notwithstanding their now being comparatively smaller in population and productive output, relative to the nation as a whole, than they were one hundred years ago before the great New Deal era and postwar westward migrations and industrializations.

Is simply adding rather than shuffling too profligate? No. It is of course true to say that in many spheres of activity there is genuine scarcity such that one must in consequence literally *reallocate* if one would *redistribute*. But that is less true in any domain in which 'more is [unambiguously] better' and admittedly necessary, such that the need of further resourcing itself is acknowledged. Nor is it true in any realm where the decider is *quite well resourced*—as is, of course, the Fed, which not only literally cannot 'run out of money,' but also earns massive seignorage revenue daily through open market operations.[59] We both can and ought simply, then, just 'make more Feds.' We might even make this our answer to those recurring cries, after all crises, to 'End the Fed.' Don't 'end' the Fed. Don't even just 'mend' the Fed. No—*spread* the Fed.

The other means of redistributing the Fed, which as I say complements the first, amounts to a means of more *fully* 'spreading the Fed.' That is to close up as many interstices as remain between new and old Regional Feds by expanding the practice of opening *Branch Offices* in larger cities that lack their own Regional Feds. The Fed System already does this, of course, but it does so anything but adequately. There is no Fed presence at all, for example, in the State of Hawaii. Yet Hawaii will likely be, of necessity, one of the most significant users, on a per capita basis, of the new Fed facilities. If we do not end up opening a Honolulu Fed, then (if we do, I'd like to spend a sabbatical there), then at the very least the San Francisco Fed or a future Los Angeles Fed should keep a Branch Office there.

Only in this general manner will we close all the smaller gaps that remain after we close the larger ones with more Regional Feds. Unless, of course, more of our states charter public banks more or less on the celebrated Bank of North Dakota model, which then themselves work in collaboration with their relevant Regional Feds. These banks could then both afford nonprofit banking services to all, and assist the Fed

Regional Banks in identifying appropriate recipients of Fed liquidity assistance—as the BND itself has done in such stellar fashion in recent weeks, outperforming all other banks of all kinds in getting PPP money to businesses.[60]

At least as importantly in the longer term, they could also assist the Fed Regional Banks in rediscovering their original mandate. For that was, again, to assist with the financing of *productive primary* market investment—investment that enables every American to improve her individual and our collective material life—not gambling on price movements in secondary financial and tertiary derivatives markets. That is of course the subject of the previous Chapters, and how to do it legislatively can be found in the Appendix below.[61]

Our aim, again, must be to reinstate the Fed's original role as a two-tiered public capital manager comprising both (a) at the 'macro' level, a Federal Reserve Board tasked with modulating monetized credit aggregates economy-wide, and (b) at the 'micro' level, Regional Federal Reserve Banks tasked with allocating public capital only productively, not speculatively, as befits that network of regional development banks which the Fed System's second tier was originally meant to be.

It should be noted in this connection that we lost sight of *both* the Fed Board's top-tier macro-modulatory, *and* the Regional Feds' bottom-tier allocative, purposes in the decades preceding 2008. Not accidentally, this was also the period when 'macroeconomics' all but disappeared as 'a thing' in highbrow economics circles, during which the understandable methodological imperative to harmonize macro- and microeconomics was mistaken for an imperative simply to jettison macroeconomics in the name of microeconomics.

It is sound to demand harmonization—indeed, this is precisely what our observations above of sound modulation's dependence on sound allocation in effect indicate. But it is foolish—and amounts to junk science—to count the obliteration of B as the harmonization of A and B. For in this realm, to jettison B is to jettison A as well. We cannot well modulate if we don't well allocate.

The *Macroprudential Turn*—that is, the revival of 'macroprudential,' or 'systemic risk,' regulation—since 2008 signals at least some renewed appreciation, which until forty years ago was commonplace, that the macro-modulatory function both can be and must be discharged. That is a genuine advance upon Greenspanian quietism, which as an offshoot of Baby Boom era (Ayn-) Randianism was simultaneously 'Austrian' in its abdication of parental guidance and Spockian (*Dr.* Spockian) in its open-handed parental indulgence. (The aforementioned 'Greenspan Put' was the central banking equivalent of an ever-larger allowance paid teenagers with no lawn-mowing or other productive chore conditionality.)

The only problem with the post-2008 Dodd-Frank modulatory revival is that it will not work absent a complementary *allocative* revival of the kind to which this Book is dedicated. You might have noticed that 'capital' market indices have equaled or surpassed past records in recent years, even as job quality in payment terms, and now a pandemic, have deprived these market heights of any 'fundamental' justification sounding in production rather than endogenous-money-fueled speculation. There is your most recent indicator of good modulation's dependence on good allocation. The Greenspan Put has become the Powell Put. And unlike Greenspan, Jay Powell has no alternative until we get allocation right. Hence...

Productive Regional Fed lending will have once again to take both of the forms it originally took. Those both were and will once again be: (a) direct purchases of productive project-associated paper issued by local and regional 'operating companies' (producers and service-providers); and (b) indirect lending to operating companies through public and private sector community banks that fund lending not with deposits, but through Fed Section 13 Discount Window lending. Both (a) and (b) will be conditioned *ex ante* on projects' promising to be productive, not speculative. And they will 'prioritize' labor-owned and labor-codetermined firms – firms whose boards or counterpart governing bodies are selected in whole or in part by labor.

The reasons for doing this are multiple. One is the tendency of returns to capital to dominate those to labor, which is macroeconomically unsustainable unless capital ownership is widely distributed. Another is what I'll call Republican Dignity—a deeply held value from the time of our republic's founding through the time of Abraham Lincoln's assuming leadership of the newly formed Republican Party. Pursuant to this ideal, labor should own or rent capital rather than being owned or rented *by* capital. Finally, yet another reason for prioritizing labor-owned or –codetermined firms is that the original justification for capital's owning or renting labor rather than the other way round in the first place—namely, perceived eighteenth- and nineteenth-century 'capital scarcity'—simply isn't 'a thing' any longer. Public capital's having become the dominant form of capital over a century ago ended that.

We can and must, then, restore and re-localize public allocation of public capital, and we should do so both (a) in the interest of production over speculation, and (b) in the interest of labor's self-determination over labor's exploitation. I call this, as noted above, a matter of 're-distributing,' as in '*again distributing*,' the project-lending of the Fed over the full breadth of our continent-spanning Republic, via the Regional Feds in the interest of labor and business alike as originally intended. Our mantra must be, as this Book's title suggests, to *Spread the Fed*.

We already 'spread' the Fed's investment-relevant data-gathering and data-analysis functions this way. It's why the Regional Feds all, in the words of my Research Assistant, 'write papers and stuff.' These papers are aptly oriented toward regional conditions over which the Regional Feds have jurisdiction. The problem is that they can be only so useful when provided in effect only for private sector financial institutions. For as noted above, these latter are simply incapable, thanks to the CAPs and ReCAPS to which they are subject, of doing anything useful—that is, productive, not speculative—with Regional Fed research. Regional Fed research is in that sense 'all dressed up with no place to go'—at least until we revive these Feds' regional development roles.

What we must do, then, is to reassign Regional Feds the tasks of lending (a) directly to local and regional enterprises, especially labor-directed and –codirected such enterprises, through public purchase of private business paper, and (b) indirectly to the same through discount lending to community, public, and other local investment institutions.

All such lending must be conditioned *ex ante* on planned projects' promising to produce real goods and services, not yet more gambling or hedging opportunities, of which there are more than enough. It should also be done in a manner that fosters and encourages labor-owned and –codetermined firms. Things would accordingly look as depicted in Fig. 7.1, with 'Liabs' abbreviating 'liabilities' and 'DW' abbreviating 'Fed Discount Window.'

Skeptics who claim that one 'can't really distinguish' between productive and speculative investment at the margin must be dismissed with a smile. For one thing, most projected investments are not 'marginal' in this sense, and in any event we can 'err on the side of inclusion' when times are tight and 'on the side of exclusion' when things are overheating. For another thing, most Regional Fed research is into

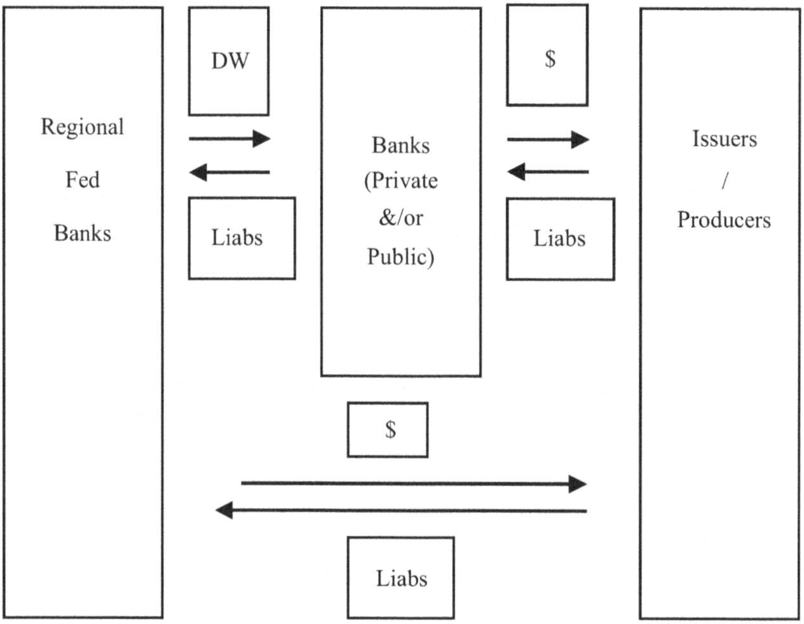

Fig. 7.1 Reformed bank/ 'spread fed' / producer relations

straightforwardly productive opportunities, not gambling opportunities—few if any institutions are better suited to spotting these than the Regional Feds.

This prospect will be easier if integrated with a more fulsome revitalization of our nation's institutions of public finance laid out in draft bill provided in the Appendix below as The National Reconstruction and Continuous Development Act, a version of which is now before Congress with the sponsorship of Rep. Ro Khanna in the House and Sen. Marco Rubio in the Senate. The bill rests on five pillars: an FSOC style National Reconstruction & Development Council ('NRDC') in the White House, an upgrade to the Federal Financing Bank ('FFB') housed in the Treasury, and a system of Universal Digital Wallets ('Digital Greenbacks') administered by the Fed and the Teasury, all briefly described in this Book's Conclusion; the Spread Fed laid out above; and a Price Stabilization Fund ('PSF,' or 'People's Portfolio') for the collaring of Systemically Important Prices & Indices, as laid out in Chapter 8, to which we now turn.

Notes

1. See, e.g., Arthur M. Schlesinger, *The Crisis of the Old Order, 1919–1933: The Age of Roosevelt*, Volume I (2003).
2. Probably still the most evocative portrait of this time is John Steinbeck, *The Grapes of Wrath* (1939).
3. See, e.g., Ira Katznelson, *Fear Itself: The New Deal and the Origins of Our Time* (2010). See also Ira Katznelson, *When Affirmative Action Was White: An Untold History of Racial Inequality in Twentieth-Century America* (2003).
4. See Schlesinger, supra note 1.
5. Id.
6. See again Hockett, *Ten Years On*, supra.
7. Id.
8. Id. Also Hockett & Dillon, *Income Inequality and Market Fragility*, supra Chapter 3 note 5.
9. See Guy Standing, *The Precariat—The New Dangerous Class* (2013).
10. See, e.g., Robert Hockett, 'Choose Your 'Socialism,'' *Forbes*, February 20, 2020.
11. See, e.g., sources cited supra.
12. Id.
13. See, e.g., Bertram Gross, *Friendly Fascism: The New Face of Power in America* (1980).
14. Comparisons of Jackson to mob-baiting Caesar are something of a hearty perennial in American history. See, e.g., Barbara Melton, *Appropriations of Cicero and Cato in the Making of American Civic Identity*, in Classics in the Modern World: A Democratic Turn? 79–88 (Stephen Harrison & Lorna Hardwick, eds., 2013).
15. See, e.g., Nancy McLean, *Democracy in Chains: The Deep History of the Radical Right's Stealth Plan for America* (2017). Also Jane Mayer, *Dark Money: The Hidden History of the Billionaires Behind the Rise of the Radical Right* (2017).
16. See, e.g., Vera Bergengruen & Brian Bennett, 'The Trump Administration's Many Vacancies Could Complicate Its Coronavirus Response,' *Time*, February 27, 2020; Nancy Cook, 'Trump's Staffing Struggle: After 3 Years, Unfilled Jobs Across the Administration,' *Politico*, January 20, 2020.

17. See, e.g., sources cited id. Also Tina Nguyen, 'Trump's Cabinet of Cronies, By the Numbers,' *Vanity Fair*, December 27, 2016.
18. See sources cited supra, notes 17and 18.
19. See, e.g., Robert Hockett, *White Paper: How to Use the Military to Produce the Supplies America Needs to Fight the Coronavirus*, New Consensus (March 2020); Robert Hockett, *Immediate Coronavirus Economic Mitigation Measures*, New Consensus White Paper (March 2020). See also Robert Hockett, 'Managing Coronavirus's Economic Fallout: Demand and Supply Side Measures,' *Forbes*, March 16, 2020; and Robert Hockett, 'Our Corona Response's Missing Ingredient: Mobilize the Supply Side!,' *Forbes*, March 18, 2020; Robert Hockett, 'The U.S. Must Take Equity Stakes in the Companies It Rescues,' *Financial Times*, March 28, 2020; Robert Hockett, 'We're at War and Need Wartime Institutions to Keep Our Economy Producing What's Necessary,' *The Hill*, April 4, 2020; Robert Hockett, 'The U.S. Must Tackle the Coronavirus Pandemic with a Playbook Out of the Great Depression and World War II, Not the Financial Crisis of 2008,' *Business Insider*, March 29, 2020.
20. See, e.g., Robert Hockett, 'Welcome to Community QE: Now Let Us Put it To Use,' *Forbes*, April 9, 2020; Robert Hockett, 'Community QE: An April Game Plan for States and Cities,' *Forbes*, April 12, 2020.
21. See sources cited id. Also Robert Hockett, *Memorandum: Community QE: Key Provisions and a 'Game Plan for Immediate State Action*, 13 April 2020, available at https://papers.ssrn.com/sol3/papers.cfm?abstract_id=3574157; Robert Hockett, *Memorandum: Community QE2: New Key Provisions and an Updated 'Game Plan' for State and Municipal Action*, 3 May 2020, available at https://papers.ssrn.com/sol3/papers.cfm?abstract_id=3589851. and my memos.
22. See 116th Congress, The Coronavirus Aid, Relief, and Economic Security ('CARES') Act of 2020, full text available at https://www.congress.gov/bill/116th-congress/senate-bill/3548/text?q=product+actualizaci%C3%B3n.
23. See Board of Governors of the Federal Reserve System, *Press Release: Federal Reserve Takes Additional Actions to Provide Up to $2.3 Trillion in Loans to Support the Economy*, April 9, 2020, available at https://www.federalreserve.gov/newsevents/pressrele

ases/monetary20200409a.htm. In what follows the terms 'City,' 'Locality,' and 'Municipality' are used more or less interchangeably to refer to what the law labels 'municipal corporations.' The terms 'Subdivision' and 'Political Subdivision' are in turn used to embrace both entities of that first type and Counties, which the new Facility described in this Memorandum distinguishes and treats differently from Cities.

24. I capitalize 'States' and 'Cities' when channeling the Fed on MLF because the MLF Term Sheets of April 9 and April 28 did so, in effect rendering the words terms of art for MLF purposes.
25. See CARES Act, supra note 22.
26. See *FRA Section 13. Powers of Federal Reserve Banks*, available at https://www.federalreserve.gov/aboutthefed/section13.htm.
27. See Board of Governors of the Federal Reserve System, Term Sheet: Municipal Liquidity Facility, April 27, 2020, available at https://www.federalreserve.gov/newsevents/pressreleases/files/monetary20200427a1.pdf.
28. See MLF Term Sheet, supra note 27.
29. Id.
30. Id.
31. Id.
32. Id.
33. Id.
34. Id.
35. See, of course (if you must), Ron Paul, *End the Fed.*
36. See generally Hockett, sources cited supra note 20.
37. Id.
38. Id.
39. Id.
40. Id.
41. See MLF Term Sheet, supra note 27.
42. See again Hockett, sources cited supra, note 67.
43. Id.
44. Id.
45. See Board of Governors of the Federal Reserve System, Term Sheet: Paycheck Protection Program Lending Facility (Apr. 9, 2020).
46. See Board of Governors of the Federal Reserve System, Term Sheet: Main Street New Loan Facility 1–2 (Apr. 30, 2020); Federal

Reserve, Term Sheet: Main Street Expanded Loan Facility (Apr. 30, 2020).

47. Id.
48. See again Hockett, sources cited supra, note 67.
49. Id.
50. Id.
51. Id.
52. See again Hockett, *A People's Fed*, supra.
53. See again Hockett, sources cited supra, note 20.
54. Id. See also, e.g., Robert Hockett, *Paying Paul and Robbing No One: An Eminent Domain Solution for Underwater Mortgage Debt*, Federal Reserve Bank of New York: Current Issues in Economics and Finance, Volume 19, No. 5 (2014), available at https://www.newyorkfed.org/research/current_issues/ci19-5.html; and Robert Hockett, *'We Don't Follow, We Lead: How New York City Will Save Mortgage Loans by Condemning Them*, 124 Yale L. J. 131 (2014).
55. See Testimony of Robert Hockett: Improving Financial Institution Supervision: Addressing Regulatory Capture, U.S. Senate, Committee on Banking and Financial Institutions, November 21, 2014, available at https://www.banking.senate.gov/imo/media/doc/HockettTestimony112114FICP.pdf.
56. See again supra, Parts I and II.
57. See again Hockett, *A Republic of Producers*, and other sources cited supra Part I, note 2.
58. See, e.g., sources cited supra, note 27.
59. See again Hockett, *Capital Commons*, supra Part I, note 2.
60. See Andrew Van Dam, 'North Dakota Businesses Dominated the PPP. Their Secret? A Century-Old Bank Founded by Radical Progressives,' *Washington Post*, May 15, 2020.
61. See again Hockett, *A People's Fed*, supra.

CHAPTER 8

Distributing Over Markets Alongside Regions: The Federal Reserve, Other Reserves, and SIPI Collaring

Abstract This Chapter turns from geographical (re-) distribution to broader market distribution of Fed modulatory activity. It first reprises my theory of what I have long called 'Systemically Important Prices and Indices'—'SIPIs'—and then shows how a buttressed Fed can modulate non-fundamentals-rooted swings in those markets. It shows that certain foodstuff, fuelstuff, and other commodity market prices are subject to massive volatility rooted in the same sorts of recursive collective action problems and related market failures introduced earlier in the Book rather than fundamentals, and that these instabilities radiate economy-wide owing to the systemic significance of those prices themselves. Since this is the reason for Fed modulatory activity in the money markets themselves, the Chapter argues, the Fed must now employ open market operations in these additional markets along with the money markets Here too, ironically enough, we shall be returning to Fed origins. For the idea of a 'reserve' implicit in the Fed's origin as a liquidity reserve now is as important an idea to recapture and act upon in other markets whose prices are SIPIs as it is in the money markets the Fed presently acts upon. Fortunately, moreover, the Chicago Fed's new trading desk near the nation's principal commodities exchange—the MERC—will enable the Fed to do here what it's long done from its New York trading desk just off of Wall Street. The Chapter shows how to do it.

R. C. Hockett, *Spread the Fed*,
https://doi.org/10.1007/978-3-031-72051-2_8

Keywords Anks · Bubbles · Busts · Central Banking · Chicago Fed · Chicago Fed Trading Floor · Chicago Mercantile Exchange · Collective Action Problems · Commodities · Commodity Derivatives · Commodity Futures · Commodity Stores · Credit · De-Industrialization · Department of Agriculture · Derivatives · Dollar · Endogenous Money · Exogenous Money · Federal Reserve System · Federal Open Market Committee · Financialization · FOMC · Graham · Graneries · Great Depression · Keynes · Liquidity Reserves · MERC · Monetary Policy · New York Fed Trading Desk · Open Market Operations · Panics · Productivism · Productivist Central Banking · Recursive Collective Action Problems · Secondary Markets · SIPIs · Speculation · Reserves · Strategic Petroleum Reserve · Strategic Reserves · Systemically Important Prices and Indices · Tertiary Markets · Underlying

The wholesale financialization of developed economies over recent decades has brought us a world in which nearly every spot market has a financial market correlate.[1] It has also brought, via the price-volatility and associated short-termism that financialization encourages, ***productive atrophy***[2] and ***deindustrialization*** to these same economies. Investment dollars for decades have flowed more toward speculative betting on price swings[3] in secondary and tertiary financial and derivatives markets, and less toward productive-capacity-building[4] in primary markets.

After a decades-long slumber, erstwhile developed economies appear at long last to be ***noticing***[5] the dysfunctions that untrammeled financialization has wrought. Socio-political volatility stemming from long-term deindustrialization and associated income- and wealth-skewing,[6] and vital supply-chain disruptions stemming more recently from the pandemic have been spurring efforts to 'build back better,'[7] 'greeinfy'[8] obsolescent technologies and infrastructures, and restore some semblance of citizen control[9] over nation-states' economies.

These productive revitalization efforts, along with geopolitical developments rooted in them, are now finding expression in the monetary realm. In so doing, they are rendering more prices than money rental (i.e., interest) rates and even more supply inputs than foodstuffs and fuelstuffs (mainly, but not solely, grains and petroleum)—what I long ago christened 'systemically important prices and indices' (SIPIs).[10] The upshot is that we shall soon have to marry our public ***liquidity*** reserves (a.k.a.

central banks), which modulate *money* supplies[11] to collar prices generally, with our public *commodity* reserves (a.k.a. 'strategic stockpiles'), which modulate *staples* supplies to collar prices more particularly.[12]

Public liquidity reserves act to modulate one obvious systemically important price: namely, the aforementioned interest rates. They collar these prices,[13] in turn, 'Goldilocks' style—not too high, not too low—by modulating supplies[14]: *money* supplies. Public *commodity* reserves do something similar: they modulate supplies of systemically important *materials* to collar *their* systemically important prices.[15]

We tend not to notice the role of commodity reserves when supplies are abundant and prices are correspondingly stable—as they were for most of the 'real' economy's 'Great Moderation' of recent decades, at least in the U.S. and its peer nations.[16] Until recently, accordingly, commodity reserves' stability-maintenance role had gone largely forgotten for decades. Steady supplies on the 'real' side of the economy during that Great Moderation kept prices within bounds. Our strategic reserves' supply modulation activities were thus less salient than those of the central banks, then seeking to stabilize anything *but* moderate *financial* markets.[17]

Another cause of our having forgotten strategic reserves in recent decades is that, via a strange sort of regulatory counterpart to financialization itself, we have for decades been treating *all price* problems as *central bank* problems,[18] forgetting the mutual interactions of *supplies* with prices. This was in keeping, of course, with a more general forgetfulness about the central importance of production itself. It was as if financialization, by projecting[19] all spot markets into derivatives markets, had dissolved[20] fiscal and industrial into monetary policy too.

Recent developments, however, have rendered this reduction, and with it our present division of 'reserve'-keeping labor, no longer tenable.[21] On the liquidity reserve side of the divide, supplies, and production are once again salient.[22] And *with* them more *prices* become salient[23]—at least in a monetary exchange economy like our own. That makes Federal Reserve operations more complex and difficult. Whether it fully appreciates the point or not, it now must specifically consider the prices of all critical inputs to production,[24] not just of 'goods and services' generically conceived. It must, in the terminology I am employing in this book, 'spread' its operations to more markets than money markets.

Meanwhile, the same financialization that obscured and undercut U.S. national *production* for decades, which largely occurred *during* the 'real' economy's putative Great Moderation, has made it more difficult for our *commodity* reserves to do *their* job too. The spot markets in which these reserves operate have morphed into a 'dog' that's now largely 'wagged' by the 'tail'[25] of financialization's chief offspring: the derivatives markets.

The upshot is obvious: just as *financialization* has now integrated our spot and derivatives markets,[26] so must *we* now integrate the operations of our price- and supply-modulating public *reserves* operating *within* those markets. We must partly merge, in other words, *Federal* Reserve operations with our *commodity* reserves' operations. This will be needed to keep both supplies and their price correlates collared—what the Federal Reserve Act and counterpart central bank mandates call 'stable.'

Central banks and strategic stockpiling agencies will accordingly no longer be able to operate 'on separate tracks'[27] in isolation from one another. They will have to *conjoin* or *coordinate*[28] their financial and spot market operations in the name of *combined* price and supply stability[29] in respect of *all* critical inputs and prices. As the world re-polarizes and developed economies repudiate post-, and embrace now post-post-, industrialization, this need will grow clearer and more compelling.

The object of the price and supply interventions that I predict will not be 'price controls.' Rather, it will be price- and supply-*pushes*, in *market-contrarian manners*, by macroprudentially authorized instrumentalities working to collar supply and price volatility rooted more in hedging and sheer speculative activity than in supply- and demand-'fundamentals'—rooted, that is, more in what the nineteenth-century political economists would have called 'exchange values' than in 'use values.'[30] The object, in other words, will be to maintain stable background conditions as is (a) requisite to long-term planning, hence productive incentives, on the part of private sector market agents, (b) now imperiled as never before in the past eighty years by geopolitical tectonic-shifting,[31] and (c) mandated by most central bank enabling legislation.

This was all destined, I think inevitably, to come to pass. And it is helpful to *understand* this if one is to understand why what I propose in this Chapter is no mere ad hoc response to a temporary problem. For what I propose is the unavoidable culmination of an evolutionary process[32] toward whose endpoint we have been stumbling with dim awareness for decades now.

Central banks are, again, originally in part *liquidity* reserves. The Fed's name reveals it. Commodity reserves are, for their part, essential *staples* reserves. Liquidity reserves become *necessary adjuncts* to commodity reserves only as a *generic* exchange economy takes on the more specific form[33] of a *monetary* exchange economy. When the latter occurs, what the political economists called exchange values—a.k.a. prices—can get out of sync with their underlying use values, thereby distorting production and consumption decisions by misleading deciders as to what is really wanted and what is available.[34] Call this 'the First Divergence.'

This divergence becomes all the more perilous as a monetary exchange economy becomes a 'financialized' economy, in which real productive inputs and consumption goods take on not only *monetized* lives as 'input and consumption good prices,' but also *financialized* lives[35] as contingent claim (a.k.a. derivative) prices. Markets become objects of 'meta-markets,'[36] which in time become objects of 'meta-meta-markets,'[37] and so on, as what I call market stratification[38] continues apace.

As this process unfolds, the use-value/exchange-value gaps of the First Divergence can be 'levered' to absurd proportions at which prices lose any discernible anchor in anything long-term or fundamental; this separates people, through secondary and tertiary market prices, from their own products and from their very means of biological survival.[39] Call this 'the Second Divergence.'

Central banks as liquidity reserves are well suited to handle the First Divergence, while central banks whose mandates are magnified into more general 'macroprudential' or 'financial stability' mandates are well suited to handle the Second Divergence.[40] But these gambits—central banks as liquidity reserves and macro-modulators—work only under two conjoined conditions.

First, the leadership of the central banks must *understand* these mandates, as, for example, the post-1935 U.S. Fed certainly did not from the late 1980s until recently and still only dimly discerns.[41] Second, central banks must *coordinate* their activities with those of the *commodity* reserves from which they evolved and to whose functions they remain nearly always and everywhere functionally tied—a requirement that cannot be understood till the first requirement is met.[42]

This Chapter aims to facilitate that understanding, and to design an institutional response. It proceeds as follows ...

Section 8.1 reprises the notion of SIPIs mentioned above in this Book's earlier Chapters. We have long recognized one such price and accordingly authorized one instrumentality to 'target' it—money rental, a.k.a. interest, rates—targeted by Fed open market operations conducted by Fed's District Bank in New York. My argument is that interest rates are now far from alone.[43] Moreover, I argue, certain *commodity* prices are more systemically important than many other SIPIs, rivaling even *home* prices in the magnitude and ubiquity of their influence.[44]

Section 8.2 turns to the financial practice of collaring in essence, the retention of price fluctuations within stable bands.[45] I note that New York Fed open market operations are collaring operations and argue that such operations are now needed in multiple additional markets—and, for reasons and in ways laid out above and especially in Chapter 7, will best be conducted by other Regional Feds in whose jurisdictions the relevant markets operate.

Against this backdrop, I highlight the signal importance of the Chicago Fed's (FRBC's) late 2022 opening of a trading floor on Wacker Drive next to the Chicago Mercantile Exchange (CME, a.k.a. 'Merc')—the world's primary commodity derivatives market—analogous to the New York Fed's trading desk just off of Wall Street.[46] I emphasize commodity prices in particular in this connection and indicate how the FRBC can rationally and transparently set the requisite commodity price collars.

Section 8.3 then pivots to strategic stockpiling agencies such as the U.S. Department of Agriculture's (USDA's) Commodity Credit Corporation (CCC)[47] and the U.S. Department of Energy's (USDOE's) Strategic Petroleum Reserve (SPR).[48] These will have to coordinate closely with the Federal Reserve Bank of Chicago (again, 'FRBC,' or 'Chicago Fed') in light of both (a) derivative prices' links to supplies in commodity markets, and, relatedly, (b) the fact that commodity derivatives traders must have at least some capacity to make and take delivery of commodities as adjuncts of their derivative trading activities.

These and related entities both in the U.S. and elsewhere, I argue, are accordingly no longer mere 'rainy day funds.'[49] They are destined to become critical *supply*-collaring entities just as the Fed and its counterparts are, complementarily, *price*-collaring entities. That will be, moreover, a return to historical practice—indeed, not only historic early Fed practice but even pre-monetary, *ancient* historical practice.

Section 8.4 then argues that these reserves must *not* now, however, be run *separately from central banks*. First, the derivatives exposures that the central banks must now undertake necessitate *some* complementary *delivery*-making and -taking capacity in associated *spot* markets—the stockpiling agencies' bailiwick, as noted above.[50] Second, the *supply*-modulating function of the *latter*, in turn, is *far easier to manage* if paired up with counterpart price-collaring in the derivatives markets by central banks. In this sense, I reinforce, from the supply side, my earlier arguments in respect of the price side of the 'marriage' that I am here urging.

Section 8.5 then consolidates the foregoing reflections and hazards predictions concerning the seemingly ever more rapidly crystalizing future. The world appears, I suggest, to be entering a new axial period involving great geopolitical competitions for newly needed industries and industrial resources, as well as associated domestic supply and price stability, worldwide.[51] If that is right, then my arguments are not only timely, but apt to require updating at least annually if not quarterly.

8.1 Central Banks and Systemically Important Prices

Let us start with a question. What is the Fed, as Federal *Reserve*, *for*? What do central banks, a.k.a. liquidity reserves, generally 'reserve'?

Most central banks have multiple functions, but one *core* function is well captured by a key phrase in the U.S.' central bank's, the Fed's, enabling act: to maintain 'stable prices.'[52] The Fed seeks to maintain stable prices to prevent serious inflations, like those of the 1970s and earlier, or deflation, like that of the 1870s, 1890s, 1930s, or 2010s.[53]

Noticeably, the Federal Reserve Act does not include any limiting language to suggest *what* '*stable* prices' it refers to.[54] The Act just says 'prices.'[55]

How should we understand this word 'prices,' then? Let us think about that; some prices seem to be more consequential than others, precisely because they feed into many *other* prices on the economy's supply side, or because they are prices of *critical human necessities* (e.g., food, water, shelter) on the economy's demand side.[56]

Consider energy prices, which determine the production and delivery costs of nearly *all other* goods and services in our economy.[57] The same is true for wage rates and salaries.[58] Food prices for their part determine how well-nourished a population is, while heating oil (which is also energy) and housing prices determine whether some people survive the winter.[59] Labor rental prices determine the costs of all things produced or supplied by working people, not to mention the level of effective consumer demand that keeps profits accumulating and workers working.

I call these prices systemically important, precisely because their significance reaches beyond the markets in which they are determined; [60] they 'spill over,' and they generate what economists call 'externalities.' Think of them by analogy to the large, interconnected 'too big to fail' banks and other financial institutions we call systemically important—the systemically important financial institutions[61] (SIFIs), hardened into a regulatory category over a decade ago by the Dodd-Frank Act passed in response to the debacles of 2008.[62]

Indeed, remind yourself that some *benchmarks and indices*—that is, *averages* of prices commonly used as broad measures of market conditions, like Libor,[63] SOFR,[64] the Consumer Price Index (CPI)[65] or Dow Jones Industrial Average (DJIA)[66] —can *also* be systemically important in the ways just elaborated. A clear analogy to Dodd-Frank's systemically important financial institutions can be seen: just as there are SIFIs, there are *SIPIs*[67]—systemically important prices and indices.

Why are SIPIs worth bringing up (again) now, especially given that I've brought them up often for well over a decade and a half?[68]

SIPIs are worth bringing up because the systemic importance of certain *particular* prices is once again salient[69]—indeed a matter of urgent and still-growing public concern. I am referring to what financiers call commodities—foodstuffs, fuel-stuffs, and certain production-critical metals and minerals. Prices of all these essentials— that is, these SIPIs— have been very volatile of late.[70] Their highs have been very high, their lows very low, and the rate of this vertigo-beckoning fluctuation has been as margin-account-draining as head-spinning.

Moreover, and somewhat ironically in view of longstanding and widespread assumptions that 'stable prices' per the Fed's mandate refer simply to CPI inflation, the Fed is in fact not very good at controlling goods and services price inflation given its present toolbox, and even when it does affect these it tends to overshoot thanks to long lag-times between rate changes and Core price changes. The Fed is far *more* influential—and more immediately so—on *commodity* prices (generally excluded from so-called 'Core' consumer price inflation measures), via the asset price channel. In other words, commodity prices, like housing and financial asset prices, are quite directly affected by Fed policy tools thanks to these tools' immediate effects on the cost of capital.

Not only is the Fed better situated to influence commodity prices than Core consumer goods prices, but commodity prices are also of *greater moment* than are other SIPI cases, which by definition are already broadly important. There are three mutually reinforcing reasons for this.

The first reason stems from commodities' tripartite role as consumer goods, productive inputs, and—thanks to their financialization in the secondary and tertiary markets—(short-term but indefinitely rollable) capital assets and hedging vehicles. (Note that the first and third roles also came to be shared, over the course of the 1990s, by real estate and its associated instruments, the heightened systemic significance of which asserted itself to catastrophic effect circa 2008.)

The second reason stems from the fact that commodities on global markets are priced in terms of the de facto global reserve currency—the U.S. dollar, issued of course by the U.S.' (for now) primary inflation-fighter, the Fed. And the third reason stems from the fact that commodity supplies are particularly vulnerable to short-term exogenous shocks and related externalities—wars, civil unrest, stochastic weather events, wildfires, and the like.

Commodities' vulnerability to supply shocks and their pricing in dollars, combined with their tripartite 'real' and financial functions as just described, accentuates the feedback dynamic characteristic of all recursive collective action problems. Indeed, it can sharpen the tragedy that these amount to. The cycle typically unfolds as follows.

First, an exogenous event—an invasion of an energy hub and/ or 'breadbasket' country in east-central Europe, say—crimps supplies, generates expectations of crimped supplies, or both. Second, owing to commodities' systemically critical role as ubiquitous inputs, the real or expected supply shock fuels expectations of general price rises. Finally, in light of inflationary expectations, financial demand for commodity derivatives (as inflation hedges) rises, generating yet further upward pressure on prices.[71]

The longer this feedback process continues, of course, the further prices depart from 'fundamental' drivers (long-term supply and demand trends), and the greater the increment of price that is attributable to credit-fueled hedging or speculation. And since, again, commodity prices enter into most other prices, that ever-growing increment of price attributable to speculation generates ever-greater *general* inflation. At some point the issuer of the currency in which commodities are priced—the Fed, issuer of the dollar—finds itself compelled to short-circuit the cycle by in effect 'killing the patient:' that is, raising rates generally, economy-wide.

It is important to recognize that while 'fundamentals'[72] play obvious roles in determining these prices in the *long* run and in *catalyzing*[73] recursive cycles in the *short* run, they are *not* the primary *drivers* in the short run. There is no *fundamental* reason that Brent Crude would sell for $100 a barrel today, $140 a barrel tomorrow, and $80 a barrel one week hence, for example. Rather, high-frequency fluctuation happens because rational portfolio hedgers and high-roller speculators with cheap credit in thin markets—more like cliques[74] than like marketplaces—*make* prices move by *hedging* against their moving or *betting* they will move, in effect prophesying outcomes in a self-fulfilling manner.[75]

Of course, fundamentals also provide *contexts* in which short-term hedging or betting behavior can be or look to be *justified*. Indeed, from speculators' point of view *pretexts are crucial* if one is to 'tell a story'[76] about her speculative purchases and thereby persuade others to follow so that she can then benefit pyramid-style or in less savory ways. There are many such stories available now—war in the breadbasket[77] known as Ukraine, sanctions on the oil well[78] known as Russia, supply chain disruptions[79] wrought by the plague known as Covid,[80] and moves on the rare earth metals[81] crucial to green industry by the geopolitical rivals known as the U.S.[82] and China.[83]

These are important true stories. But they are never the whole story. Indeed, once the financial 'tail' flips to 'wagging' the real economy 'dog,' they are not even the *relevant* story.

Some readers will remember when oil prices reached new record highs in the spring and summer of 2008.[84] Some blamed tensions, then war, between Russia and Georgia. Others observed that the world had reached 'peak oil '—new discoveries cannot 'keep pace with the decline in existing reserves' and hence prices would now rise.[85] Counterpart remarks had been made to explain record housing price rises in the decade or so before 2006—Ricardian marginal lands theory combined with Malthusian population theory to 'prove' prices 'could only go up.'[86]

That was nonsense then[87] and it is nonsense now.[88] The *backstory* is seldom the *now* story; it is the 'someday' story. What, then, is the story now, and what does the Fed got to do with it?

At present we are witnessing dramatically destabilizing price volatility in multiple commodity markets[89]—maybe more at one time than we have ever seen before. And the chaos is hardly confined to just one or a few countries—it is worldwide.[90] Wheat and other grain prices are spiking and plunging and spiking and plunging everywhere.[91] Oil prices are doing likewise. So too, though somewhat less visibly, are prices of metals and minerals now vital to new green industries growing in China, Europe, and even Stateside. In all these cases long stories can be told—the stories I hinted at several paragraphs back.

But again, these are more *backstories* than *the* stories. *The* stories include speculative trades done with erstwhile Quantitative Easing (QE)-enabled cheap borrowings and privileged information[92]—the kind of information enjoyed by well-connected traders on thin markets—markets that function in large part as clubs rather than circuit-boards. Add endogenous credit-money[93] of the QE variety to these places, and you get what I have elsewhere dubbed recursive collective action problems[94] (again, 'ReCAPS' for short) out the proverbial wazoo—you get 'vicious circle'[95] volatility with respect to prices that neither we, nor, increasingly, even lesser traders[96] can afford to watch gyrate or stagger.

Of course, as Quantitative Tightening ('QT') now takes effect and once erstwhile-abundant liquidity dries up, 'the' story will change course. But this will be thanks to the central bank's response to the previous real story, a response that makes use of the principal instrument—alas, a blunt instrument—that the Fed has at its present disposal: suppressive balance sheet shrinking and rate-hiking. Now, why is this *publicly* problematic, and again what does my proposed augmentation of the Fed's toolkit with more granular instruments got to do with it?

Well, it is publicly problematic because all these prices are, as just discussed, SIPIs.[97] They are systematically important[98] in the senses I rehearsed earlier, and extra systemically important at that, for the additional reasons that I just laid out.

Wheat and other grain prices both are prices of essential comestibles[99] and inputs to other prices. Their rising causes calories falling—people are poised to go hungry this year. Petroleum prices[100] of course affect both production and transportation—including transportation of consumer goods—ubiquitously, as we have not yet transitioned to green. Meanwhile metals and minerals prices slow that transition itself, by making it much more expensive, if not impossible, for as long as they are driven up artificially—that is, speculatively.[101]

And owing to their roles as financial instruments as well as 'real' inputs, they are subject to yet greater feedback effects than are other SIPIs.

8.2 Stability Maintenance Through SIPI-Collaring

Here is where my proposal for a new Fed commodity facility comes in, along with the Department of Agriculture's Commodity Credit Corporation (CCC) and the Department of Energy's Strategic Petroleum Reserve (SPR). And not just them, but also their counterparts worldwide, working through their global coordinating bodies the Bank for International Settlements (BIS) and the International Energy Agency (IEA), for starters.

When a price fluctuates wildly in the short-term, when long-term 'fundamental' value is simply a mean toward which prices tend over time but from which they depart quite dramatically up and down day to day, there is reason to 'collar' them[102] close to that mean—at least if the prices are SIPIs and market failures are readily seen to be why they are short-term volatile. And there is no better collarer than the central bank. Its balance sheet and literally infinite liquidity[103] within its jurisdiction enable it and only it to ride out the liquidity crunches that attend bipolar speculative thrill-rides in commodity markets.

What do I mean here, specifically? I mean this: the Fed and other central banks must begin designating certain prices and indices 'systemically important,'[104] using criteria analogous to those that Dodd-Frank does in designating SIFIs.[105] They must then undertake to counter-speculate against the speculators who drive SIPIs fleetingly above and below their longer-term mean values, shorting them when speculators are over-long, going long when speculators are over-shorting.

The object must be to keep these prices nearer to so-called 'Core' prices, as tracked in measuring 'Core Inflation,'[106] any time peak-to-trough amplitudes cannot be explained by reference to fundamentals but can be by reference to dramatically asymmetric information, market power, or very cheap credit.

Maybe this sounds radical or unfamiliar to you, a revolutionary departure from precedent. It should not, and it is not. Consider two familiar examples.

One global market with club-reminiscent properties much like those of commodity markets is the foreign exchange market,[107] with few traders, asymmetric information, lots of cheap QE-money to gamble with, etc. Central banks understand this, while also understanding that wildly fluctuating currency values are profoundly destabilizing—the kind of craziness that gets you trade breakdown and World War II.[108]

So the world's central banks, Fed included, manage what they call a 'dirty float' regime,[109] intervening in the markets for the currencies they themselves issue to manage fluctuations within reasonable bounds—that is, collars. Swap lines introduced since the 2008 crash[110] further enhance the arrangement. Nobody thinks this radical—not anymore.

One more example—every weekday morning, women and men at a Lower Manhattan trading desk[111] read sets of instructions composed for them the night or early morning before. These instructions have been developed on the basis of reams of market and trading information digested in the previous hours, with a view to determining what the demand for money is apt to be in the coming hours. As the sun rises over the East River, these traders will begin trading, and will be trading all day. And they will be doing it for the U.S..[112]

I am describing the New York Fed trading desk,[113] whose personnel are executing instructions attributable to the Federal Open Market Committee (again, 'FOMC'), which oversees Fed open market operations in Treasurys and Treasury repo.[114] The Fed does this to collar another systemically important price bearing on broad price stability—the money rental, a.k.a. interest rate. That is right—*stable* prices per the Federal Reserve Act are *collared* prices,[115] collared because they are, whether generally articulated in this manner or described less pellucidly, SIPIs.

But how to collar commodity prices, you ask? Well, start with this data-point: what New York is to money prices, Chicago is to commodity prices,[116] at least in the U.S. and nontrivially beyond. The Chicago Mercantile Exchange (again, 'Merc,' or 'CME') on and near Wacker Drive is to commodities and their derivatives much what the New York Stock Exchange and Big 6 banks are to money and securities on and near Wall Street. And lo, as I discussed in January 2022,[117] the Chicago Fed now has a new trading facility[118] virtually identical to—indeed set up in part by personnel from—the New York Fed's trading unit.[119]

Has this new facility gone up because the Fed agrees with me here? Well, maybe, seeing as how I pushed this idea incessantly while working there over a decade ago.[120] But I doubt it. I suspect that the Fed has figured this out on its own, for it is obvious once you think about it and Fed personnel are typically both brilliant and well versed on all markets that affect price stability. The Fed and its peers worldwide will be collaring commodities, if not by this year, then soon.[121]

How might this work? It will be helpful, I think, to start with the price-collaring part of the story here, then turn to the complementary supply-collaring correlate below in 8.3. While the latter will be handled by the aforementioned USDA CCC and USDOE SPR in coordination with the Federal Reserve Board (FRB), Federal Open Market Committee (FOMC), and the FRBC, the former will be handled by the FRBC in coordination with the aforementioned four agencies.

The first thing to note about this new FRBC role is that it will amount to maintaining a collar, hence a combined call and put, for designated commodities. I call these 'Covered Commodities'—essentially, those covered by the statutory or regulatory provisions that provide for the operations I am here proposing.

For Fed collar-setting not to generate perverse consequences, and, more affirmatively, for the tool to work optimally in a manner that puts even private speculators to good use, we will first want a transparent means of setting what I will call 'the Presumptive Collar.' The Presumptive Collar will be the Collar that is maintained absent some plausible 'fundamentals'-based explanation for a price's departure from Core.

The best trigger location for purposes of setting the Presumptive Collar will, then, work a provisional 'cut' between possible fundamentals-based explanations for price movements on the one hand and pure feedback-based explanations for the same on the other hand. For the reasons already given, the simplest way to locate this cut is to track persistent divergences between what I will call Covered Commodity Prices—simply the prices of Covered Commodities—and Core consumer goods prices as tracked by standard Core inflation and deflation measures.[122]

Once a protracted divergence between Presumptive Collar prices and Core prices emerges, the second step for the FRBC to take is to ascertain the cause or causes of the divergence—again with a view to whether there might be some plausible 'fundamentals'-based explanation for the divergence. A sudden loss of Saudi petroleum production capacity wrought by Iranian nuclear attack on its wells, for example, or a catastrophic drought across North America, would obviously bear upon actual rather than merely expected or hedged commodity supplies. The same is true in the other direction, a macroeconomic contraction that temporarily dampened demand.

Cases of this sort might well warrant emergency action of various kinds to aid hard-hit constituencies or tide-over emergencies but would not warrant narrow collar-maintenance—at least with respect to those 'real' components of price change. By contrast, where hedging or speculation in response to such events, or to lesser events like the 2008 war on Georgia or the current war on Ukraine, represent large portions of the relevant price swings, some degree of collaring will be in order.

In general, the greater the part that 'fundamentals'-based causes play in constituting departures from Core prices by Covered Commodity prices, and the smaller the part therefore that speculation does, the wider should be the collar. Symmetrically, the less that fundamentals-rooted phenomena account for the changes and the more therefore that speculation does, the narrower should be the collar.

Over time, we should expect the FOMC and FRBC to develop ever-more nuanced means of disaggregating causal components of price changes and planning its purchases and sales on the commodity markets accordingly. That is, after all, what the FOMC and the Federal Reserve Bank of New York (again, New York Fed, or FRBNY) have done in respect of other price changes to which present-day FRBNY open market operations in Treasury securities are conducted.

But even at this early stage, the FRBC, which has gifted and able staffers following and seeking explanations for commodity price movements in keeping with its research department functions, will be working with much more than a blank slate. It will hardly be flying blind—as its aforementioned activity, now underway, to establish its own FRBNY-reminiscent trading desk strongly suggests that it knows.

It might nonetheless be objected that putting the Chicago Fed in the commodity trading business will expose it to new kinds of risk that do not afflict New York Fed open market operations in Treasury Securities. Sellers of puts and calls in derivatives markets, after all, sometimes must take or make actual deliveries of underlyings. Is the Fed now equipped to do that?

This is of course where the other component of my proposal—the role of our federal strategic commodity reserve agencies—comes into our story. The move that our central banks must make now is also a move that demands reconnection with counterpart entities acting less in financial than in spot markets. I refer now to strategic reserves.

8.3 SIPI-Collaring's Supply-Collaring Correlate: Strategic Reserves

There is one risk that might reasonably be thought to attend the collaring strategy just advanced—the risk that, in some cases, central banks might actually have to take or deliver possession of actual physical commodities in settling derivative contracts. Is this a worry? No, for here is where our already-existent strategic storage agencies step into the picture.

The *Federal* Reserve is not the U.S. *only* 'Reserve.' There is also a *Strategic Petroleum* Reserve, multiple *foodstuff* reserves, and sundry *metals* and *medicine* reserves. What is strategic about these, and in what sense is *their* reserve activity reminiscent of *Federal Reserve* activity?

This is obvious once you think about it, which until now we have had less obvious reason than we have now to do. What central banks—recall, *liquidity* reserves—are to what I call Systemically Important Prices and Indices, or SIPIs, *commodity* reserves are to what I will call 'Systemically Important Supplies and Inputs,' or SISIs.

Indeed, in an important sense this latter now-under-appreciated category is both functionally and historically prior to the former still-under-appreciated category. For the former is only the latter as manifest in a monetary exchange economy and hence in time a financialized economy.

This is a very long story, alas, but a story that bears brief retelling here. I will stick to bare-bones, recounting only what is needed to see the importance of now linking liquidity reserves—that is, central banks—with commodity reserves.

Off to the races…

Most in 'the West' know the Biblical story of Joseph.[123] The proverbial father of nations advised Egypt's Pharaoh to store grain over seven fat years to provide for a soon-to-come seven lean years. The counsel proved wise, and both Joseph and his descendants were richly rewarded. Some of us also know counterpart stories from elsewhere in the world. The most familiar is probably that of Qing Dynasty China's (seventeenth-twentieth century) institution of the ever normal granary.[124] These were maintained by imperial mandate in all provinces for essentially the same purpose as Joseph's reserve. It is a familiar idea, rooted in the commonsense wisdom of 'saving for a rainy day.' Cultures everywhere seem to have variants. We are a wise species.

What many might be *less* aware of than these rainy day funds for both literal and figurative 'rainy days,' however, is the fact that strategic stockpiles in market-based ***monetary-exchange*** economies[125] like those we now live in offer an ***additional***, albeit related, promise. They offer means of eliminating the principal Achilles Heel that afflicts all exchange economies—hence both capitalism and market socialism[126] —themselves: the twin problems of frequent over- and under-production.

In effect, strategic stockpiles of adequate size are great means of collectively addressing the most poignant—indeed, often lethal—collective action challenge afflicting all systems of decentralized market exchange. And while that is always the case and hence always worth remembering, the present now seems an especially apt time for recollection. For again, we are now face-to-face with a new set of crises[127] that are partly rooted in our having forgotten.[128]

A market economy is a set of arrangements under which people produce not for direct consumption, but for exchange. You make, in other words, not what you will eat, wear, or use, but what you can sell to earn money to purchase from others what you will eat, wear, or use.

That, we now know after centuries of experience, is an immensely productive mode of organization, at least in potential. It is history's way of incenting us beyond mere subsistence-level production. For when you produce to do more than consume, you begin to see possibilities beyond current consumption. And so society in aggregate comes to produce more and more, not just quantitatively speaking but also qualitatively speaking. That is one reason that even Marx celebrated market exchange's achievements up to his time.[129]

There is one vulnerability that comes with this functional separation of production and consumption, however. It is a vulnerability that lies at the root of nearly all of capitalism's growing pains in the nineteenth and twentieth centuries and most of its crises even now.

You see, if people are not directly producing to consume, they do not know immediately how much to produce. There is no automatic coordination,[130] we might say, of production with desired or potential consumption as there would be were we each to produce all and only that which we wished to consume.

Hence there is always the prospect that uncoordinated producers will over-produce or under-produce in aggregate—thereby bringing on either a glut that removes profit opportunities and hence incentives to produce or a shortage that brings monetary inflation and hence incentives to hoard.

Therein lies the root of capitalism's two principal species of periodic crisis—'great' depressions (suggestively also called debt-deflations[131]) and 'hyper'-inflations.[132] The first stems from *over*-production rooted in imperfect coordination of production and consumption; the second stems from *under*-production rooted in imperfect coordination of production and consumption.[133] And both manifest, as the correlate terms deflation and inflation suggest, in price changes in any monetary exchange economy.[134]

Modern societies have developed two means, thus far, of addressing the coordination challenge posed by exchange economies' separation of production and consumption. They amount, in effect, to polar extremes, neither of which is foolproof. And strategic stockpiling, we will see, amounts to a Goldilocks or Golden Mean solution, in the parlance of Southey or Aristotle, respectively.

To start with the polar extremes, the two means of coordination to which I refer are *central planning* and *the price system.*

The idea behind central planning, popular in twentieth-century socialist societies, is familiar.[135] A planning board acting in the name of the citizenry sets broad production goals for satisfying citizens' consumption needs.[136] It then allocates tasks across society's productive units to meet those goals.[137] These then aim to meet quotas assigned in the plan—not unlike the separate production units within large multi-factory business conglomerates[138] in modern capitalist societies.

Planning has historically performed well at avoiding what nineteenth-century political-economists called general gluts[139] (overproduction) thanks to its non-reliance on profit incentives—incentives that individually drive more production but collectively can bring over-production. But it has fared less well at avoiding the opposite problem (underproduction),[140] as well as the related problem of misallocation[141] (overproduction of X1, X2, X3, underproduction of Y1, Y2, Y3).

The *reason* for central planning's shortcomings is sometimes taken to justify its polar opposite— 'the [so-called] *price system.*'[142] Optimal coordination of production and consumption, it is said, requires aggregation of immense quantities of information concerning scores of millions of citizens' consumption preferences and budget constraints. No central planning body, it is then noted, can possibly gather and analyze such volumes of information in order to match aggregate production to consumption demand.

Only a market possessed of certain structural features, price system advocates conclude, can impound so much data and thereby coordinate supplies with demands. The requisite features are those of the Smithian invisible hand,[143] as more rigorously, axiomatically defined by the Nobel Prize winning Arrow-Debreu[144] models to most academic economists.

Disagreements over these competing claims drove the great socialist calculation debate[145] of the early mid-twentieth century. Here economists like Ludwig von Mises and Friedrich Hayek argued that only *markets* can 'calculate' in the requisite way by amalgamating sufficient quanta of information. Followers of Kläre Tisch, Enrico Barone, Oskar Lange, and Abba Lerner for their part claimed it was only a matter of time before supercomputers would develop sufficient capacity to outperform markets in coordinating production with desired consumption.

If you are familiar with current developments in computing technology, algorithmic trading, and the uses that massive *private* sector central planners like Wall Street's investment banks make of the same, you might think the computing enthusiasts had a point. Arrow, Debreu, and their many followers, after all, speak of planners.[146] And their models are far too abstract to give guidance as to how they are best implemented, be it by markets or planners or supercomputers.

The impression that the planners might not have been all wrong might be further strengthened when you reflect on the fact that the price mechanism has flaws of its own. Notable among these are proclivities toward the opposite problem of central planning's—that of overproduction, hence glut-wrought revenues short of production costs. This results in producer insolvencies and worker redundancies, which then bring further contractions in sales, hence more layoffs and bankruptcies and so on.

These are the crises that we call recessionary spirals, debt-deflations, or depressions. And *another* decorated economist, Joseph Stiglitz,[147] earned *his* Nobel precisely by showing that markets that *are not* possessed of the Arrow-Debreu properties—which indeed no market is—cannot be assumed to yield that optimal coordination of production and consumption which Smith's invisible hand does.

The past several decades suggest Stiglitz's point is important. For present purposes, however, we can view the jury as still out on modern markets' and modern computing's significance for the 'great socialist calculation debate.' For the far more exciting point for *my* purposes is that societies *long ago* developed non-purely planning, non-purely market means of addressing the coordination challenge posed by the separation of production and consumption. And it is a means that amounts to the extremes-straddling *Golden* Mean to which I alluded before.

I refer to the strategic stockpiling story with which I began—the story of Joseph and Pharaoh and Qing China's ever normal granaries.[148]

To see how such stockpiling —that is, the maintenance of more reserves than a Fed-style bank liquidity reserve—amounts to a Goldilocks alternative to the unsatisfactory extremes of pure centralization and decentralization, note two things about reserves that tend to go overlooked: (a) first, what we might call their productive smoothing, or buffering function; and (b) second, the fact that *production*-smoothing in *monetary-exchange* economies, where *prices* rather than *plans* mediate between consumption and production, translates into *price*-smoothing.

To start with the first point, one way to view Joseph's counsel to Pharaoh is as a counsel of smoothing—of what engineers will call amplitude modulation and financiers call collaring[149] or volatility-buffering.

The premise behind lean years and fat years is that in the former not enough is produced while in the latter more than enough is produced. One thus smoothens the cycle—they narrow the spread—between surplus and deficit by holding the surplus *in reserve* and then filling the deficit with it once a dearth opens. One thereby affords both continuity of adequate consumption and certainty as to that adequacy going forward.

This is precisely why you encounter words like both buffer and reserve in contexts where volatility familiarly threatens. The *Federal* Reserve[150] began as a public bank-liquidity pooling mechanism—a liquidity reserve—for run-prone banks. The United States Strategic *Petroleum* Reserve[151] bears its name for a similar reason. The capital buffers[152] we require our banks to maintain likewise enable our savings institutions to absorb portfolio losses. And so on. These are all tools for *cabining volatility*.[153]

8.4 Integrating Financial and Spot Market 'Reserves:' Why and How

Turning next to the second point, that volatility of the sort that smoothening smoothens is *particularly* dangerous in societies, like ours, in which *prices* mediate between consumption preferences and production decisions. Any distortions that find their way into the price system can cause both (a) collectively perverse consumption and production *decisions* and even (b) lost consumption and production *capacity*. In that sense, price system vulnerabilities threaten production and consumption themselves—the very stuff of continued existence.

How, you might ask? A producer who receives a price signal suggesting more demand for a product tomorrow than actually materializes might overproduce. They might in fact do so to the point that they cannot recoup costs via sales. Our producer might then in consequence face insolvency and hence lay off workers who thus lose their purchasing power and thereby shrink demand further; this then leads to more lost sales and bankruptcies and so on, in the familiar vicious circle of deflationary spiral. The same can, of course, happen in reverse, where distorted price signals prompt underproduction that issue in *inflationary* spirals.

In other work, as noted above, I call these 'spiral' structures recursive collective action problems[154] (again, ReCAPS for short), to which decentralized exchange economies are especially prone. Collective action problems, recall, are situations in which individually rational actions aggregate into collectively irrational outcomes.[155] A recursive such problem is one with feedback effects, where each market outcome feeds back into and amplifies the very process that has produced it.[156]

Examples are abundant.[157] Depressions (again, a.k.a. debt-deflations[158]) and hyperinflations as just noted are cases in point. So are bank runs, asset price bubbles, and asset price fire sales, as noted earlier. Outside of market contexts, arms races and common tragedies are structurally similar stories. In all such cases, the individually rational thing is the collectively irrational—even tragic, calamitous—thing.

Now the way you solve a collective action challenge is to act collectively. You authorize a collective agent[159] who can act in the name of us all to address the problem that people in their individual capacities lack authority, capacity, and hence sufficient incentive to address.

We have a name for collective agents of this kind: governments.[160] And what I am about to show is that strategic stockpiling— tellingly done in the past by collective authorities like governments—is an optimal mode of collective address of that poignant coordination challenge I have said afflicts all exchange economies. And that optimal spot market mode is itself optimized through integration with its modal correlate in the financial markets—derivative price-collaring as discussed above.

A few quick examples, some historic and some futuristic, should suffice to make the point appreciable. Let us look first at foodstuffs and fuelstuffs again and then at some presently uncertain but promising new technologies of the kind apt to figure importantly in the industries of tomorrow.

For millennia, agriculture has been subject to great uncertainty. (It is no accident that Egypt's and China's stories above concerned grain.) For one thing there is weather. For another there are oft-changing tastes. And finally, in market economies there is decentralization of production, whereby one farmer does not know what other farmers are doing. Under such circumstances, two risks afflict a society's very ability to feed itself.

One risk is that farmers in aggregate harvest too much, thereby driving down prices and bankrupting themselves—classic overproduction rooted in collective action challenge. The other is that farmers, mindful of that very risk, hold back in planting or form a cartel—classic underproduction or illicit collective agency that risks unaccountable market power of the kind antitrust laws are meant to prevent.

How does a large enough, publicly administered granary[161] resolve this conundrum? Easy: It *purchases* excess when farmers collectively overproduce. Also, it *sells* surplus when weather or illicit collusion bring either natural shortages or artificial shortages of the kind we call 'market-cornering.' But it also does something else: because prices mediate production and consumption in monetary-exchange economies, the granary's provision of *supply* stability is also, potentially, the provision of *price* stability. To smoothen supply volatility is likewise to help modulate price volatility.

In light of the outsized role played by commodity derivatives markets in driving commodity prices as described above, however, supply modulation alone will not always suffice to effect price modulation. Happily, however, central bank collaring of *derivative* prices can do the trick—provided that central banks have delivery-making and -taking capacity. But that is just what public commodity reserves do have the capacity to do. *Integrate* central bank price-collaring with commodity reserve supply-collaring, then, and we are 'golden.'

Turn next to fuels. While these are not subject to stochastic weather conditions as foods are, they are subject to like forms of risk—notably new discoveries and wars in the regions where fuels are extracted. And, as with foodstuffs, in market economies there is decentralization of production, whereby one driller or refiner does not know what all other drillers or refiners are doing. Under such circumstances, two risks afflict a society's ability to transport and power itself.

One risk is that drillers and refiners in aggregate extract or refine too much, thereby driving down prices and bankrupting themselves—again classic overproduction rooted in classic collective action challenge. The other is that drillers and refiners, mindful of that very risk, hold back in drilling or refining, or form a cartel—again classic underproduction or illicit collective agency that risks unaccountable market power of the kind antitrust law is meant to prevent.

How does a large enough public fuel reserve[162] resolve this conundrum? Easy: It purchases excess when drillers or refiners collectively overproduce. And it sells surplus when war or illicit collusion brings either stochastic shortages or artificial shortages of the kind we call 'market-cornering.' But, like the granary, it also does something else: again because prices mediate production and consumption in monetary-exchange economies, the fuel reserve's provision of supply stability is also at least a partial provision of price stability. To smoothen supply volatility is likewise to help modulate price volatility.

Owing again to the outsized role played by commodity derivatives markets in driving commodity prices as described above, however, supply modulation alone will not always suffice to effect price modulation. Again—*integrate* central bank price-collaring with commodity reserve supply-collaring, then, and again, we are 'golden.'

One more example. Suppose that nearly all in society know that the future belongs to some new industry or industries[163]—say, solar panels, windmills, heat pumps, semiconductors, and/or electric vehicles (EVs). Suppose also that great uncertainty attends both the speed with which demand for the new industries' products will grow and the rate at which sundry producers will start to produce, and that similar uncertainties afflict supplies of essential inputs to the products that these industries will produce—rare earth metals, by way of now-salient example.

Under such circumstances, two risks again afflict a society's move to adopt, adapt to, and disseminate the technologies with all deliberate speed—technologies which, again, I am positing that all understand will be justifiably dominant *some* day.

One risk again is that producers in aggregate manufacture too much, thereby driving down prices and bankrupting themselves—again classic overproduction rooted in classic collective action challenge. The other risk is that our producers, mindful of the first risk, hold back in producing, or form a cartel—classic underproduction or *illicit* collective agency that risks unaccountable market power of the kind antitrust law is meant to prevent.

What sort of public action might effectively mimic a reserve or a granary to solve this conundrum? Easy: the public contracts to procure any reasonable excess that new manufacturers collectively overproduce, perhaps even *using* the surplus to provision non-wealthy sectors or segments of our economy or population that cannot afford to adopt new technologies quickly. And it *sells off* surplus on a nonprofit basis if unforeseen market changes or illicit collusion bring either stochastic shortages or artificial shortages of the kind we call 'market-cornering.'

Like both the granary and the petroleum reserve, the public also does something *else* under this scenario: because prices mediate production and consumption in monetary-exchange economies, the public's provision of supply stability is also a partial provision of price stability. To smoothen supply volatility is likewise to provide means to modulate price volatility. And whatever margin of price stability remains to be publicly managed through collaring in the derivatives markets, the public *can* manage through one or more of its regional Fed district banks—which ones to ride on depends on which regions the products in question substantially trade on.

Here, then, we see concretely how my proposal to integrate USDA CCC, USDOE SPR, and other U.S.' strategic reserve operations—e.g., rare earth metal, semiconductor, and/or medical supply reserves—with FRBC, FRBNY, and possibly other FR district bank operations, as described in 8.2, gets real traction.[164] Modulating supplies will aid the Fed in modulating prices. It also will afford the Fed means of both taking and making delivery when its operations in the derivatives markets occasionally oblige it to do so in fulfillment of those puts and calls that constitute its collars.

By the same token, Fed operations in derivatives markets will aid our strategic reserves in modulating *supplies*. In effect, we get full coverage, where the all-important function of collaring, i.e., stability, is concerned, of both spot markets and, in our now nearly fully financialized world, their secondary and tertiary[165] financial market correlates.

Strategic reserves, then, are not merely rainy-day funds. They can help afford price stability itself to decentralized exchange economies that on the one hand separate, yet on the other hand must coordinate, production and consumption decisions. If they coordinate with the central bank counterparts in the financial markets, they can do everything even in financialized economies that they once did in pre-financialized economies.

'Central planning' approaches to the challenge have thus far proved wanting. But so too have 'decentralized price system' approaches. It has been said that 'central banking is the last refuge of central planners.' That is about one-quarter true. It is half true of central banks themselves, because central banks actually do their part of that minimal degree of central coordinating that even decentralized market exchange economies require to persist.[166] And it is half of that half-truth because the same is true of strategic reserves—the spot markets' indispensable counterparts of our financial markets' central banks.

The stockpiling—a.k.a 'smoothing,' 'cushioning,' 'modulating,' 'reserving' or 'buffering' —solution in effect splits the difference between the supply extremes, while the counterpart central bank 'collaring' solution splits the difference between those extremes' correlates in the financial markets. These paired solutions eschew comprehensive collective micro-planning but provide just enough collective agency in macro-modulating to insulate individual agency against collective action predicaments. Symmetrically, they eschew unbuffered exposure to the vagaries and collusion-vulnerabilities of inherently imperfect, distortion-prone price systems, but cushion against them only to the degree necessary to keep production and prices reliable through time.

Our ancient forebears in Egypt and China and elsewhere were not the only ones among our ancestors who understood this. So too did our more immediate predecessors of the 1930s and 1940s, who left institutional legacies that we still live with yet seem to have forgotten.

Vice President Henry Wallace and Benjamin Graham, for example, should be celebrated not only as FDR's Vice President and Warren Buffet's mentor, respectively, but also as advocates of a 1930s rendition of the old 'ever normal granary' for all agricultural and other volatile commodities.[167] The great yet mysteriously forgotten Cornell economist George Warren—he of Commodity Dollar renown, along with Fisher, during the New Deal—should be likewise remembered.[168]

J.M. Keynes, meanwhile, should be celebrated not only for theorizing the importance of countercyclical fiscal and monetary policy to smooth macro-business-cycling,[169] but also for pushing—with Wallace, Warren, and Graham—a global commodity store to act as a worldwide granary alongside his postwar World Bank and International Monetary Fund, the former proposed as a global rendition of the U.S.s' Federal Reserve.

We live with these visionaries' legacies to this day. The USDA's Commodity Credit Corporation (CCC)[170] was formed in the early 1930s to stabilize agricultural prices for producers and consumers alike. The USDOE's Strategic Petroleum Reserve (SPR)[171] was formed immediately after the oil shocks of the early 1970s for similar purposes, though the cartel known as OPEC makes its job harder than the CCC's. The SPR also works in global coordination with counterparts worldwide through the auspices of the International Energy Agency (IEA).[172]

And the U.S. military maintains incipient stockpiles of strategic metals, minerals, and medical materials—a legacy of the 'preemptive buying' and 'preclusive purchasing' programs begun by the Roosevelt Administration at the outset of the Second World War in the late 1930s.

This is happening all of the time, yet we seldom notice until, in crises, leaders announce high-profile releases of 'government cheese' as did President Reagan in 1981,[173] and President Biden in autumn 2021 and spring 2022.[174] I fear, though, that we are at a point where we no longer can live with benign neglect of these critical instrumentalities.

We must afford the Fed means of modulating crucial commodity prices. That means we must also afford it the Chicago Fed means of both taking and making delivery of underlyings when its operations in the commodity derivatives markets occasionally oblige it to do so in fulfillment of those puts and calls that constitute its collars. Our existing reserves, providentially established during our earlier periods of marked volatility during the 1930s and 1970s, are *the* means of doing so.

Our form of capitalism going forward is going to be far more dependent on all of these and counterpart mechanisms—operating at much larger scale. And the easiest method of levering *current* scale up to *requisite* scale is by combining these spot market functions with counterpart derivatives market functions of the kind discussed earlier in Parts I and II.

Why do I speak of greater need for these things going forward? That takes us to this Chapter's final Section.

8.5 What Happens Now?: Post-'Post-Industrialism'

Back to the question: Why do I say we will have greater need for the integrated mechanisms that I have been proposing here going forward?

Well, is it not obvious? Russia's invasion of Ukraine—a breadbasket and fuel crossroads of all Eurasia—in early 2022 upended global food and fuel markets,[175] bringing both price spikes and great volatility that working people in particular, but also economies more generally, can ill afford. The invasion is also catalyzing geopolitical, military, and trade realignment on a massive scale,[176] with Europe, the Anglosphere, and many Asian nations suspicious of China drawing closer together, China and Russia effectively combining, and middle powers like Turkey and Iran seeking separate courses.

Competition for resources seems sure to follow these realignments, particularly because geopolitical competition is better understood now to require geo-*economic* and hence geo-*productive* competition. The U.S., like other early-developing countries that rationalized globalization-wrought productive decline as a somehow mysteriously better 'post-industrialism,' are now seeing the error of their ways and moving to re-industrialize in a new era of what we might call 'post-post-industrialism.' They are doing so by leapfrogging forward toward the predicted industries of tomorrow.

These industries of tomorrow that are emerging today, discussed just above in the previous part, will require materials that, as the phrase 'rare earth metals' itself suggests, are rare. China is already cornering—some now say hoarding—supplies of these materials, while also stockpiling fuels and grains. The rest of the world is sure to follow, both in the name of security and in the related name of post-post-industrialism.

These moves will bring ever-worsening uncertainties to supplies of vital materials worldwide. That includes everything from the aforementioned foods, fuels, and rare earth metals[177] to less rare but still able to be cornered inputs like silicas.[178] And this is to say nothing of essential medicines, medical equipment, and all-important ubiquitous manmade inputs to widely needed products—advanced microprocessors being the most urgent[179] case in point.

Meanwhile, recent Covid-wrought supply chain disruptions and the aforementioned sharpening of geopolitical rivalries have now also highlighted the signal imprudence of overreliance,[180] not only on some other national *governments* for foodstuffs, fuel stuffs, and all crucial inputs[181] to the industries of today and tomorrow, but also reliance on lengthy, multimodal *transport* networks. Even apart from now sharpening geopolitical and geo-economic rivalries, in other words, the very physics, geography, and meteorology of extended supply chains means more precarity in a world of pandemic and catastrophic climate change.

All these uncertainties of course magnify through derivatives trading into extreme price volatility as elaborated above in 8.2 and 8.3. The U.S.

and other countries can ill afford these supply and associated price instabilities. The supplies and their associated prices will have to be collared and can only be collared by the means proposed here in this article.

The U.S., to its credit, has incipient facilities[182] and initiatives underway in all these areas at this instant. I noted the new trading facility being established at the Chicago Fed, and likewise noted the U.S.' strategic stockpiling programs left over in attenuated form from the volatile 1930s and 1970s.[183] Yet these programs and facilities thus far are *only* incipient and are not proceeding at anywhere near the requisite scale and requisite speed.

If we seriously wish to modulate energy prices during our potential green transition[184] and productive renewal[185] even after the Ukraine war, then, our SPR will need much more than 700 barrels of crude oil to work with in buying and selling to discharge its smoothing mandate. And if we wish to do likewise with foodstuffs, metals, microchips, and medical materials, our CCC and our military will have to up their games massively too.

China has adopted our old playbook in this realm and pursues it as we once did. So rapidly has it stockpiled foods and fuels and so decisively has it moved toward cornering global rare earth metals supplies that observers unflinchingly now say, as noted above, that it is actively hoarding.[186] The last time we saw stockpiling on this scale was, ominously, *also* in Asia: Japan did it back in the 1930s, in preparation for war.[187] The U.S. responded quite quickly[188] back then, pursuing a vigorous program of preclusive buying and storing.[189]

There is good news, however, where scaling is concerned. Why? Because much of what only large physical capacity can do in the spot markets can be synthetically done in the derivatives markets—especially by any entity with effectively infinite liquidity and a massive balance sheet. And there is one entity possessed of both attributes: the United States Federal Reserve.[190]

If we use current CCC, SPR, and counterpart storage capacities as fallback delivery-taking and –making facilities attached to Chicago Fed commodity derivatives trading,[191] then, as I am proposing here, we can do much of the price-stabilizing that is now growing ever more urgent. We can do so even with *current* physical capacity.

This is not, however, to recommend not *expanding* those physical capacities. There are urgent domestic *supply* needs even apart from the distinct, though related, price-collaring needs rooted in supply volatility.

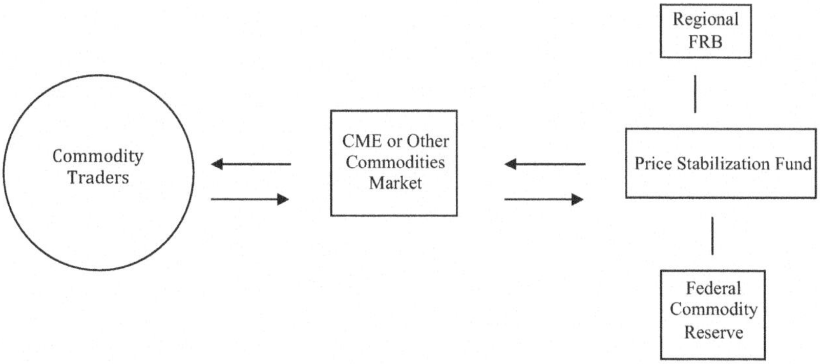

Fig. 8.1 Combined fed/commodity reserve & commodity market flow structure

The actionable point here, then, is that we should build out and fill up all physical storage capacity as quickly as possible, while not waiting before commencing to price-collar in the derivatives markets. Indeed, proceeding in this fashion—starting with price-collaring through operations on the Merc—will smoothen the supply-building process itself.

We can capture what I have laid out here diagrammatically as follows (Fig. 8.1):

Notes

1. Robert C. Hockett, *The Wealth of Our Commonwealth: Money and Capital in the Productive Republic* 10–16 (Cornell L. Sch. Legal Stud. Rsch. Paper Series, Rsch. Paper No. 21–48, 2021), https://papers.ssrn.com/abstract=3808790 [hereinafter Hockett, *The Wealth of Our Commonwealth*].
2. *See* Robert Hockett, 'Make America Make Again,' *Forbes* (May 1, 2022, 5:55 PM), https://www.forbes.com/sites/rhockett/2022/05/01/make-america-make-again/ [hereinafter Hockett, *Make America*].
3. *See* Robert C. Hockett, *Building Banks Better: A Plan to Put Public Capital Back to Public Use 2* (Feb. 1, 2022) (unpublished manuscript), https://papers.ssrn.com/abstract=4023614 [hereinafter Hockett, *Building Banks*].

4. *See* Robert Hockett, 'War On Inflation, Part 1: The Lesson Of World War II,' *Forbes* (Nov. 12, 2021, 8:58 AM), https://www.forbes.com/sites/rhockett/2021/11/12/war-on-inflation-part-1-the-lesson-of-world-war-ii/ [hereinafter Hockett, *War*].
5. *See* id.
6. Robert C. Hockett & Daniel Dillon, *Income Inequality and Market Fragility: Some Empirics in the Political Economy of Finance, Part 1*, 62:5 Challenge 354, 354–74 (2019), https://doi.org/10.1080/05775132.2019.1638026.
7. Robert Hockett, 'Building Back Better Forever: The National Reconstruction and Continuous Development Act Of 2021,' *Forbes* (Jan. 29, 2021, 10:26 AM), https://www.forbes.com/sites/rhockett/2021/01/29/building-back-better-forever-the-national-reconstruction-and-continuous-development-act-of-2021/?sh=13fb84b93cfd.
8. *See* Robert C. Hockett, *Financing the Green New Deal: A Plan of Action and Renewal xvii-xviii* (2020) [hereinafter Hockett, *Financing the Green New Deal*].
9. *See* Robert Hockett, 'Choose Your "Socialism",' *Forbes* (Feb. 20, 2020, 11:43 AM), https://www.forbes.com/sites/rhockett/2020/02/20/choose-your-socialism/ [hereinafter Hockett, *Choose*].
10. How to Make QE More Helpful: By Fed Shorting of Commodities, *Benzinga* (Oct. 14, 2011, 8:41 PM), https://www.benzinga.com/node/1988109.
11. Robert C. Hockett, *A Fixer-Upper for Finance*, 87 Wash. U. L. Rev. 1213 (2010) [hereinafter Hockett, *A Fixer-Upper*].
12. *See* Robert C. Hockett, 'The Strategy Part Of 'Strategic Stockpiling': From Mere 'Rainy Day Funds' To Disruption-Free Mass Production,' *Forbes* (June 5, 2022, 1:02 AM), https://www.forbes.com/sites/rhockett/2022/06/05/the-strategy-part-of-strategic-stockpiling-from-mere-rainy-day-funds-to-disruption-free-mass-production/ [hereinafter Hockett, *The Strategy Part*].
13. *See* Robert Hockett, 'Central Banks Can, Must, And Will Collar Commodity Prices,' *Forbes* (Mar. 23, 2022, 7:37 PM), https://www.forbes.com/sites/rhockett/2022/03/23/central-banks-can-must-and-will-collar-commodity-prices/ [hereinafter Hockett, *Central Banks Can*].

14. Robert C. Hockett, *Rousseauvian Money* 46 (Cornell L. Sch. Legal Stud. Rsch. Paper Series, Rsch. Paper No. 18–48, 2018), https://papers.ssrn.com/abstract=3278408 [hereinafter Hockett, *Rousseauvian*].
15. *See* Hockett, *The Strategy Part*, supra note 12.
16. Robert C. Hockett et al., *The Way Forward: Moving from the Post-Bubble, Post-Bust Economy to Renewed Growth and Competitiveness* (Cornell L. Sch. Legal Stud. Rsch. Paper Series, Rsch. Paper No. 12-01, 2012), https://papers.ssrn.com/abstract=1987139.
17. Robert C. Hockett, *Bubbles, Busts, and Blame* (Cornell L. Sch. Legal Stud. Rsch. Paper Series, Rsch. Paper No. 11–09, 2011), https://papers.ssrn.com/abstract=1805930.
18. *See generally* Robert C. Hockett, *The Capital Commons: Digital Money and Citizens' Finance in a Productive Commercial Republic*, 39 Rev. Banking & Fin. L. 345 (2019–2020) [hereinafter Hockett, *The Capital Commons*].
19. Hockett, *The Wealth of Our Commonwealth*, supra note 1, at 10–14.
20. Id.
21. *See* Hockett, *The Capital Commons*, supra note 18, at 351.
22. *See* Robert Hockett, 'Building Back Better' Phase Two—Time Now To Jumpstart Domestic Production,' *Forbes* (Mar. 3, 2021, 2:11 PM), https://www.forbes.com/sites/rhockett/2021/03/03/building-back-better-phase-two--time-now-to-jumpstart-domestic-production/ [hereinafter Hockett, *Building Back*].
23. Robert C. Hockett, 'Prices, Preclusive Purchases, And Production: Some Forgotten Solutions to Forgotten Inflation Problems,' *Forbes* (May 13, 2022, 6:23 PM), https://www.forbes.com/sites/rhockett/2022/05/13/prices-preclusive-purchases-and-production-some-forgotten-solutions-to-forgotten-inflation-problems/ [hereinafter Hockett, *Preclusive Purchases*].
24. Id.
25. Hockett, *The Wealth of Our Commonwealth*, supra note 1, at 30–36.
26. Hockett, *The Wealth of Our Commonwealth*, supra note 1, at 10–16.
27. *See* Hockett, *The Strategy Part*, supra note 12.
28. Robert C. Hockett, From the Federal Reserve to Strategic Reserves—and Back: A Marriage Proposal 5 (June 5, 2022)

(unpublished manuscript) (on file with the Social Science Research Network).
29. Id.
30. Robert C. Hockett, *The Macroprudential Turn: From Institutional 'Safety and Soundness' to Systemic 'Financial Stability' in Financial Supervision*, 9 Va. L. & Bus. Rev. 201 (2015) [hereinafter Hockett, *Macroprudential*].
31. *See* Christopher M. Matthews, Summer Said, & Benoit Faucon, *The End of Energy Free Trade*, Wall St. J., (June 3, 2022), https://www.wsj.com/articles/the-end-of-energy-free-trade-oil-and-gas-sanctions-russia-war-ukraine-putin-11654262659.
32. *See* Hockett, *The Capital Commons*, supra note 18, at 361.
33. Hockett, *Rousseauvian*, supra note 14, at 46–49.
34. *See* id. at 46–49.
35. Hockett, *The Wealth of Our Commonwealth*, supra note 1, at 10–14.
36. Id.
37. Id.
38. Id.
39. *See* Hockett, *Rousseauvian*, supra note 14, at 2, 45–49.
40. Hockett, *Macroprudential*, supra note 30, at 228.
41. *See* id. at 202 (explaining Greenspan's position during the 'Lean versus Clean' Debate just over a decade ago).
42. *See* Hockett, *The Strategy Part*, *supra* note 12.
43. Robert C. Hockett, *Open Labor Market Operations* 4–5 (Cornell L. Sch. Legal Stud. Rsch. Paper Series, Rsch. Paper No. 19–02, 2018), https://papers.ssrn.com/abstract=3298823 [hereinafter Hockett, *Open Labor*].
44. *See* Robert Hockett, 'Fine-Tuning Monetary Easing, Part 2: The Fed's New Chicago Trading Capacity,' *Forbes* (Jan. 31, 2022, 9:58 PM), https://www.forbes.com/sites/rhockett/2022/01/31/fine-tuning-monetary-easing-part-2-the-feds-new-chicago-trading-capacity/ [hereinafter Hockett, *Fine-Tuning*].
45. *See* Hockett, *Central Banks Can*, supra note 13.
46. Hockett, *Fine-Tuning*, supra note 44.
47. *See generally Commodity Credit Corp.*, U.S. Dept. Of Agric., https://www.usda.gov/ccc (last visited Nov. 20, 2022).
48. *See generally SPR Quick Facts*, U.S. Dep't of Energy Office of Cybersecurity, Energy Sec., And Emergency Response,

https://www.energy.gov/fecm/strategic-petroleum-reserve-9 (last visited Dec. 30, 2022).

49. *See* Hockett, *The Strategy Part*, supra note 12.
50. *See* Hockett, *Central Banks Can*, supra note 13.
51. Hockett, *War*, supra note 4; Hocket, *Preclusive Purchases*, supra note 23.
52. 12 U.S.C. § 225a.
53. Robert Hockett, 'To Reverse Inflation Today and Prevent It Tomorrow, The Fed Should Short-Sell Commodities Now As We Speed-Up Production For Later,' *Forbes* (Jan. 30, 2022, 3:40 PM) https://www.forbes.com/sites/rhockett/2022/01/30/to-reverse-inflation-today-and-prevent-it-tomorrow-the-fed-should-short-sell-commodities-now-as-we-speed-up-production-for-later/ [hereinafter Hockett, *To Reverse Inflation*]; *see* Robert Hockett, Debt, Deflation, and Debacle: Of Private Debt Write-Down and Public Recovery 4 (May 21, 2013) (unpublished manuscript), https://papers.ssrn.com/abstract=2268230 [hereinafter Hockett, *Debt, Deflation*].
54. *See* 12 U.S.C. § 221.
55. 12 U.S.C. § 225a.
56. *See generally* Robert Hockett & Roy Kreitner, *Just Prices*, 27 Cornell J. L. & Pub. Pol'y 771 (2018), https://papers.ssrn.com/abstract=3069966.
57. Hockett, *To Reverse Inflation*, supra note 53.
58. *See* Hockett, *Open Labor*, supra note 43, at 6–7.
59. Robert Hockett, *Republican Homeowning*, 62(3) Challenge 200 (2019) https://doi.org/10.1080/05775132.2019.1606541.
60. Hockett, *To Reverse Inflation*, supra note 53.
61. Daniel Liberto, *Systemically Important Financial Institution (SIFI) Definition*, INVESTOPEDIA (Aug. 14, 2022), https://www.investopedia.com/terms/s/systemically-important-financial-institution-sifi.asp.
62. *See generally* Dodd-Frank Wall St. Reform and Consumer Protection Act, Pub. L. No. 11–203, 124 Stat. 1803–09 (defining and describing systemically important financial market utilities).
63. *See generally* Julia Kagan, 'LIBOR: What the Interbank Offered Rate Is, How It's Used,' *Investopedia* (Mar. 12, 2022), https://www.investopedia.com/terms/l/libor.asp.

64. Daniel Kurt, 'Secured Overnight Financing Rate (SOFR) Definition and History,' *Investopedia* (Mar. 22, 2022), https://www.investopedia.com/secured-overnight-financing-rate-sofr-4683954.
65. *See generally* Jason Ferando, 'Consumer Price Index (CPI),' *Investopedia* (Oct. 18, 2022), https://www.investopedia.com/terms/c/consumerpriceindex.asp.
66. *See generally* Dow Jones Industrial Average, *Wikipedia* (Nov. 11, 2022), https://en.wikipedia.org/w/index.php?title=Dow_Jones_Industrial_Average&oldid=1091333199.
67. Hockett, *To Reverse Inflation*, supra note 53.
68. *See, e.g.*, Robert Hockett & Aaron James, *Money from Nothing: Or, Why We Should Stop Worrying About Debt and Learn to Love the Federal Reserve* 208–09 (Melville House, 2020); *see also* Hockett, *Building Banks*, supra note 3, at 27; Hockett, *Financing the Green New Deal*, supra note 8, at 24–25; Hockett, *The Capital Commons*, supra note 18, at 427; Hockett, *Fine-Tuning*, supra note 44; Hockett, *To Reverse Inflation*, supra note 53.
69. *See* Adam Tooze, *Chartbook #100: Must Central Banks Become Lenders of Last Resort for Commodity Markets?*, Chartbook (Mar. 16 2022), https://adamtooze.substack.com/p/chartbook-100-must-central-banks.
70. *See* Joe Wallace et al., *Cash Crunch Drives Wild Moves in Commodities*, Wall St. J. (Mar. 21, 2022), www.wsj.com, https://www.wsj.com/articles/cash-crunch-drives-wild-moves-in-commodities-11647866942.
71. The same process of course operates in reverse when exogenous events—an oil field discovery, say, or an unexpectedly high crop yield—generate the reality or expectations of supply gluts and consequent price drops. More on this prospect below in 8.3 on what the political economists called general gluts, and the policy responses thereto developed during the 1930s. *See infra* Section 8.3.
72. Hockett, *A Fixer-Upper*, supra note 11, at 1237.
73. Id.
74. Rupert Russell, *Price Wars: How the Commodities Markets Made Our Chaotic World* (Doubleday, 2022).
75. *See* Robert C. Hockett, *Recursive Collective Action Problems*, 3 J. Fin. Persp., July 2015, at 17, 27, https://papers.ssrn.com/abstract=2239849 [hereinafter Hockett, *Recursive*].

76. Hockett, *A Fixer-Upper*, supra note 11, at 1232–41.
77. *See* Geoffrey York, 'Higher Food Prices Caused by Ukraine War Spark Protests, Instability in Some Countries,' *The Globe and Mail* (Mar. 21, 2022), www.theglobeandmail.com, https://www.theglobeandmail.com/world/article-higher-prices-spark-protests-and-instability-in-fallout-from-ukraine/.
78. *See* Rakteem Katakey, 'Oil Climbs as EU Considers Beefing up Sanctions on Russian Crude,' *Bloomberg* (Mar. 23, 2022), https://www.aljazeera.com/economy/2022/3/23/oil-climbs-as-eu-considers-beefing-up-sanctions-on-russian-crude.
79. *Why Global Supply Chains May Never Be the Same - A WSJ Documentary*, Wall St. J. (Mar. 23, 2022), https://www.wsj.com/video/series/chain-reaction/why-global-supply-chains-may-never-be-the-same-a-wsj-documentary/4EFE56B6-8A1D-4478-9F88-8F055AFBF675.
80. Robert Hockett, 'Our Corona Response's Missing Ingredient—Mobilize The Supply Side!,' *Forbes* (Mar. 18, 2020, 12:29 PM), https://www.forbes.com/sites/rhockett/2020/03/18/our-corona-responses-missing-ingredient--mobilize-the-supply-side/.
81. *See* Neil Hume, 'Is There a New Supercycle in Metals and Minerals?,' *Financial Times* (Feb. 25, 2022), https://www.ft.com/content/975b92c0-8f70-48c2-8e50-f615db68228d?accessToken=zwAAAYSX8DdJkdOXW5LAj3BIwtOOUPYV22gijQ.MEUCIQDIgZx1EvGKryQV.
82. *See* Samantha Subin, 'The New U.S. Plan to Rival China and End Cornering of Market in Rare Earth Metals,' *CNBC* (Apr. 17, 2021, 9:00 AM), https://www.cnbc.com/2021/04/17/the-new-us-plan-to-rival-chinas-dominance-in-rare-earth-metals.html.
83. *See* The Editorial Board, *Opinion | A Chinese Nickel Market Mystery*, Wall St. J. (Mar. 22, 2022, 7:00 PM), www.wsj.com, https://www.wsj.com/articles/a-chinese-nickel-market-mystery-london-metal-exchange-tsinghsan-11647982954.
84. *See* James D. Hamilton, 'Causes and Consequences of the Oil Shock of 2007–08,' *Brooking Papers on Econ. Activity* 215, 215–83 (2009).
85. Will Kenton, 'What Is Peak Oil?,' *Investopedia* (June 21, 2022), https://www.investopedia.com/terms/p/peak_oil.asp.
86. Hockett, *A Fixer-Upper*, supra note 11, at 1239, 1273.

87. *See* James Smith, 'The 2008 Oil Price Shock: Markets or Mayhem?,' *Resources for the Future* (Nov. 5, 2009), https://www.resources.org/common-resources/the-2008-oil-price-shock-markets-or-mayhem/.
88. Russell, supra note 74. It seems to be forgotten now not only that hedge funds were taking outsized positions in the petroleum futures markets in the lead-up to mid-2008, but also that expectations were widespread that the dollar would plummet, which indeed it did till July. Motives to hedge portfolios with commodities in their capacities as financial assets were accordingly heightened. When the dollar then began rising over the course of autumn 2008 in response to the United States' financial meltdown, 'peak oil' was forgotten and petroleum prices cratered.
89. *See* Gabriel Friedman, *'A Wild Time': Why Commodities Are in a Supercycle of Volatility*, Fin. Post (Sept. 22, 2021), https://financialpost.com/commodities/energy/oil-gas/a-wild-time-why-commodities-are-in-a-supercycle-of-volatility.
90. *See* Rupert Russell, 'Unless We Act, Escalating Commodity Prices Will Cause a Decade of Global Turmoil,' *The Guardian* (Mar. 19, 2022, 6:17 AM), https://www.theguardian.com/commentisfree/2022/mar/19/commodity-prices-escalating-global-turmoil.
91. *See* id.
92. *E.g.*, Deconstructed Podcast: Are Prices 'Engines of Chaos'?, *The Intercept* (Mar. 18, 2022, 10:03 AM), https://theintercept.com/2022/03/18/deconstructed-prices-wars-markets/.
93. *See* Hockett, *Building Banks*, supra note 3, at 29.
94. Hockett, *Recursive*, supra note 75.
95. Harry Dempsey and Neil Hume, 'Trafigura's Finance Chief Warns of Commodity Industry Stress,' *Fin. Times* (Mar. 23, 2022), https://www.ft.com/content/264173c2-794e-423b-b345-60868265d92b.
96. *See* Mercenary Ákos, *Pozsár Zoltán: Csúnyán Lábon Lőtte Magát A Nyugat Az Orosz Szankciókkal, És Fel Nem Fogom, Ezt Hogy Nem Látták Előre*, PORTFOLIO (Mar. 16, 2022, 6:10 AM), https://www.portfolio.hu/gazdasag/20220316/pozsar-zoltan-csunyan-labon-lotte-magat-a-nyugat-az-orosz-szankciokkal-es-fel-nem-fogom-ezt-hogy-nem-lattak-elore-533009.
97. Hockett, *To Reverse Inflation*, supra note 53.

98. Id.
99. Hockett, supra note 10.
100. Id.
101. *See* Hockett, Robert, 'War On Inflation, Part 3: Resuming Leadership In High Capacity Battery Manufacture,' *Forbes* (Nov. 15, 2021), https://www.forbes.com/sites/rhockett/2021/11/15/war-on-inflation-part-3-resuming-leadership-in-high-capacity-battery-manufacture/ [hereinafter Hockett, *War on Inflation*].
102. Hockett, supra note 10.
103. *See generally* Hockett, *The Capital Commons*, supra note 18.
104. Hockett, *Fine-Tuning*, supra note 44, at 2.
105. *See generally* U.S. Dep't of the Treasury, *Designations*, U.S. Dep't of the Treasury (Nov. 13, 2022), https://home.treasury.gov/policy-issues/financial-markets-financial-institutions-and-fiscal-service/fsoc/designations.
106. Will Kenton, 'Why Core Inflation Is Important,' *Investopedia* (May 3, 2022), https://www.investopedia.com/terms/c/coreinflation.asp.
107. *See generally* Robert C. Hockett, *Bretton Woods 1.0: An Essay in Constructive Retrieval*, N.Y.U. J. Legis. & Pub. Pol'y, 401 (2013) [hereinafter Hockett, *Bretton*].
108. *See* id.
109. Id.
110. Robert Hockett, Is the Fed Jimmy Stewart? Is It the World's Central Banker?, *Benzinga* (Dec. 4, 2010), https://www.benzinga.com/node/668325.
111. Hockett, *To Reverse Inflation*, supra note 53.
112. Id.
113. Id.
114. Bd. of Governors of the Fed. Rsrv. Sys., *The Fed - Federal Open Market Committee*, Fed. Rsrv. (Nov. 2, 2022), https://www.federalreserve.gov/monetarypolicy/fomc.htm.
115. Hockett, *To Reverse Inflation*, supra note 53.
116. Hockett, *Fine-Tuning*, supra note 44, at 5.
117. Id.
118. Id.
119. Id.
120. *See* Hockett, supra note 10.
121. Hockett, *Fine-Tuning*, supra note 44.

122. It will be well for the FRBC to employ all standard measures—PCE as is standard Fed practice, but also BEA and CPI—in view of the epistemic difficulties—not impossibilities!—that attend distinguishing supply and demand 'fundamentals' from 'speculation.'.
123. *What Can We Learn from the Life of Joseph?*, Biblword (Jan. 14, 2021), https://www.biblword.net/what-can-we-learn-from-the-life-of-joseph/.
124. *See* generally Eds. Encyc. Britannica, *Ever-Normal Granaries*, Encyc. Britannica, https://www.britannica.com/topic/ever-normal-granary (last visited Nov. 20, 2023).
125. Hockett, *The Capital Commons*, supra note 18.
126. Hockett, *Choose*, supra note 9.
127. Hockett, *Preclusive Purchases*, supra note 23.
128. Id.
129. *See* Louis Menand, *Karl Marx, Yesterday and Today*, THE NEW YORKER (Oct. 3, 2016), http://www.newyorker.com/magazine/2016/10/10/karl-marx-yesterday-and-today.
130. Paul Craig Roberts & Matthew A. Stephenson, *On the Commodity Mode of Production: One More Time*, 9 J. of Econ. Issues 530 (1975).
131. *See* id.
132. *See* Hockett, *Debt, Deflation*, supra note 53, at 7.
133. *See* id.
134. *See* id.
135. *What Is a Centrally Planned Economy?* INVESTOPEDIA (Jan. 20, 2020), https://www.investopedia.com/terms/c/centrally-planned-economy.asp.
136. Id.
137. *See* id.
138. R.H. Coase, *The Nature of the Firm*, 4 ECONOMICA 386, 388–89 (1937).
139. *See* Salim Rashid, *Malthus' Model of General Gluts*, 9 Hist. of Pol. Econ. 366, 366–83 (1977).
140. Underproduction, *Merriam-Webster*, https://www.merriam-webster.com/dictionary/underproduction (last visited Jan. 30, 2023).
141. *Misallocation*, *Merriam-Webster*, https://www.merriam-webster.com/dictionary/misallocation (last visited Jan. 30, 2023).

142. *See* George J. Stigler, *Price System*, Encyc. Britannica, https://www.britannica.com/topic/price-system (last visited Jan. 30, 2023).
143. Christine Majaski, 'What Is the Invisible Hand in Economics?' *Investopedia* (Jan. 1, 2023), https://www.investopedia.com/terms/i/invisiblehand.asp.
144. John Geanakoplos, *Arrow-Debreu Model of General Equilibrium*, in 1 The New Palsgrave Dictionary of Econ. 451–65 (ed., 2018).
145. Socialist Calculation Debate, *Wikipedia* (Nov. 16, 2021, 12:07 AM), https://en.wikipedia.org/w/index.php?title=Socialist_calculation_debate&oldid=1055456431.
146. http://home.uchicago.edu/~vlima/courses/econ201/pricetext/PlanProb.pdf.
147. *See generally* David R. Henderson, *Joseph E. Stiglitz*, Econlib, https://www.econlib.org/library/Enc/bios/Stiglitz.html (last visited Jan. 30, 2023).
148. *See* supra notes 123, 64 and accompanying text.
149. *See* Hockett, *Central Banks Can*, supra note 13.
150. *See* Robert Hockett, 'The Once and Future Fed—And Treasury (Part 1),' *Forbes* (Mar. 23, 2021, 9:19 AM), https://www.forbes.com/sites/rhockett/2021/03/23/the-once-and-future-fed and-treasury-part-1/.
151. *See generally SPR Quick Facts*, supra note 48.
152. Julia Kagan, 'Capital Buffer,' *Investopedia* (May 27, 2020), https://www.investopedia.com/terms/c/capital-buffer.asp.
153. Hockett, *Macroprudential*, supra note 30, at 214.
154. Hockett, *Recursive*, supra note 75, at 1.
155. Id.
156. *See* id. at 1, 9.
157. *See generally* id.
158. *See* Hockett, *Debt, Deflation*, supra note 53, at 7.
159. *See* id. at 48.
160. *See* id.
161. *E.g.*, Eds. Encyc. Britannica, supra note 124.
162. *See e.g.*, *SPR Origins*, U.S. Dep't of Energy Office of Cybersecurity, Energy, Sec., and Emergency Response, https://www.Energy.gov/fecm/strategic-petroleum-reserve-0 (last visited Feb. 18, 2023).
163. *See* Hockett, *Make America*, supra note 2.

164. *See* supra Part II.
165. Hockett, *The Wealth of Our Commonwealth*, supra note 1.
166. Id.
167. Derk Bodde, *Henry A. Wallace and the Ever-Normal Granary*, 4 The Far Eastern Q. 411, 411–26 (1946), https://doi.org/10.2307/2049789; *see* Benjamin Graham, Storage and Stability: A Modern Ever-Normal Granary (1937); *see also* Perry Mehrling, *The Monetary Economics of Benjamin Graham: A Bridge Between Goods and Money?*, 33 J. of the History of Econ. Thought 285, 285–305 (2011).
168. *See generally* George F. Warren & Frank A. Pearson, *Prices* (John Wiley & Sons 1934).
169. *See generally* Hockett, *Bretton*, supra note 107.
170. *Commodity Credit Corp.*, supra note 47.
171. *See generally SPR Quick Facts*, supra note 48.
172. *See generally* IEA—Int'l Energy Agency, https://www.iea.org (last visited Feb. 18, 2023).
173. Erin Blakemore, *How the U.S. Ended Up With Warehouses Full of 'Government Cheese,'* History (July 26, 2018), https://www.history.com/news/government-cheese-dairy-farmers-reagan.
174. *President Biden Announces Release from the Strategic Petroleum Reserve As Part of Ongoing Efforts to Lower Prices and Address Lack of Supply Around the World*, The White House (Nov. 23, 2021), https://www.whitehouse.gov/briefing-room/statements-releases/2021/11/23/president-biden-announces-release-from-the-strategic-petroleum-reserve-as-part-of-ongoing-efforts-to-lower-prices-and-address-lack-of-supply-around-the-world/.
175. *See* John Baffles & Peter Nagle, *Commodity Prices Surge Due to the War in Ukraine*, World Bank (May 5, 2022), https://blogs.worldbank.org/developmenttalk/commodity-prices-surge-due-war-ukraine.
176. *See* Matthews, supra note 31.
177. *See* Hockett, *War on Inflation, Parts 1 through 3*, infra.
178. Robert Hockett, 'War On Inflation, Part 2: Restoring Leadership In Semiconductor Production,' *Forbes* (Nov. 14, 2021, 10:27 AM), https://www.forbes.com/sites/rhockett/2021/11/14/war-on-inflation-part-2-restoring-leadership-in-semiconductor-production/.
179. Id.

180. Hockett, *Preclusive Purchases*, supra note 23.
181. Hockett, *War*, supra note 4.
182. Anshu Siripurapu, *The State of U.S. Strategic Stockpiles*, Council on Foreign Relations (Apr. 20, 2022), https://www.cfr.org/backgrounder/state-us-strategic-stockpiles.
183. See supra 8.4.
184. *See generally* Robert C. Hockett & Rhiana Gunn-Wright, *The Green New Deal: Mobilizing for a Just, Prosperous, and Sustainable Economy* (Cornell L. Sch. Legal Stud. Rsch. Paper Series, Rsch. PaperNo. 19–09, 2019), https://papers.ssrn.com/abstract=3342494.
185. *See* Hockett, *Building Back*, supra note 22.
186. Adam Minter, 'One Reason for Rising Food Prices? Chinese Hoarding,' *Bloomberg* (Jan. 4, 2022), https://www.bloomberg.com/opinion/articles/2022-01-05/one-reason-for-rising-food-prices-chinese-hoarding.
187. *See* Hockett, *War*, supra note 4.
188. Id.
189. Hockett, *Preclusive Purchases*, supra note 23.
190. *See generally* Hockett, supra note 18.
191. *See* Hockett, *Fine-Tuning*, supra note 44.

Conclusion: The Old Made New

The once again Spread Fed will work best in tandem with (a) updated global monetary arrangements that permit unrestricted monetary policy autonomy within every sovereign polity, and (b) several complementary upgrades to existing U.S. institutions of public finance aimed at refocusing economic and financial policy on the restoration of what I elsewhere call our American 'Republic of Producers.'

The mentioned global updating—item (a)—is the subject of prior work I have published as well as of my next book, more on both of which are below. As for the upgrades to the U.S.' existing institutions of public finance—item (b)—legislation instituting these changes, now proposed in Congress as mentioned above, will be found in the Appendix below. Briefly and diagrammatically here, the emendations are as follows.

Pillar I: A National Reconstruction and Development Council

First, configure all members of the White House Cabinet who have jurisdiction over the nation's primary infrastructures and industries into a National Reconstruction and Development Council ('Council,' 'NRDC'). The Council will be Chaired *ex officio* by the President and Vice President, and officially by the Fed Chair and Secretary of the Treasury—a bit like the Financial Stability Oversight Council ('FSOC'). Its task will be to formulate and regularly update a 'National Development

R. C. Hockett, *Spread the Fed*,
https://doi.org/10.1007/978-3-031-72051-2

Strategy' ('NDS') analogous to the 'National Defense Strategy' updated each year by the nation's defense and security agencies.

The NDS will identify the sustainable industries of tomorrow that are in need of jump-starting today, and will likewise identify the most polluted and 'left-behind' regions of the country and segments of our citizenry in need of a green boost. It will earmark specific project fields and public investment projects—wind, solar, geothermal, electric …—in which to invest, since incumbent carbon-committed firms won't, to make national development both environmentally sustainable and once again never-ending.

A cardinal intellectual and policy blunder of the past 50 years has been both to segregate 'national development' from justice and sustainability, and to treat it as a one-off achievement instead of a perpetual process of technical and productive renewal. Going forward, we must remember the words of the great development economist Bob Dylan—'he not busy being born is busy dying'—and remind ourselves that these words are as true of societies as they are of individuals. The Council will be the embodiment of that recollection. And as a subset of the White House Cabinet, it will be both democratically accountable and able to plan our ongoing green development coherently instead of in 'siloed' fashion.

Pillar II: An Upgraded Federal Financing Bank

Second, use the Treasury's already-existing Federal Financing Bank (FFB) as the Council's investment arm. Currently FFB uses Congressionally appropriated funds to finance all our federal agencies through lending and credit support. Two simple tweaks, one at the intake and one at the output end, will transform FFB into a permanent and environmentally sensitive national development bank alongside the Council.

At the output end, authorize FFB to invest in sub-federal units of government, and public-private development partnerships, as well as in federal agencies as currently. Let it also take equity stakes in addition to credit instruments, where appropriate, as financing instruments. For in some cases boardroom 'voice' will be helpful in overseeing projects, and earned revenue will be welcome as well.

At the input end, authorize FFB also to issue its own credit instruments, and to form Special Purpose Trusts to fund fully diversified portfolios of specific project types. Let private sector investors purchase stakes in these funds too, so as both to add private to public capital in financing perpetual national development, and to give pension funds something more productive than Wall Street to invest in.

The World War I era War Industries Board ('WIB') and War Finance Corporation ('WFC'), as well as the World War II era War Production Board ('WPB') and Reconstruction Finance Corporation ('RFC'), paired up much as I am envisaging the NRDC and the FFB pairing up here. In the case of the earlier pairings, the US had to finance and ramp-up war production quite quickly. The aforementioned institutions accordingly planned and financed both conversion of existing factories and the establishment of new factories to produce steel, rubber, jeeps, tanks, ships and planes, taking both debt and equity stakes in the relevant firms. They financed these operations, in turn, with public capital, private capital, and retained earnings.

Today we are faced not with war, but with what the American philosopher William James called 'the *moral equivalent* of war.' Working together, then, the NRDC and upgraded FFB can, from the output end, plan and finance decarbonizing projects from municipal installation of electric vehicle charging ports at all parking meters, through the building of multiple battery and wind turbine factories in scores of impoverished communities, on down to the retrofitting of all sizable buildings in the country. And at the intake end they can form investment pools for all project types—e.g., a 'solar fund,' a 'battery fund,' a 'wind power fund,' etc.—in which anyone can invest.

Pillar III: The 'Spread Fed'

Third, 'Spread the Fed.' Americans have forgotten that the Fed was initially established as a network of regional development banks. While today the regional Fed District Banks function mainly as think tanks, in the Fed's early decades they purchased short-term commercial paper issued by small businesses and agricultural concerns. That assured adequate liquidity and short-term funding to our nation's primary drivers of technological development and productivity growth. Today the Fed doesn't operate like that, yet its enabling Act still authorizes this form of development support.

All that the Fed has to do is once again open its 'Discount Window' to businesses of the kind that it used to support, while in this case 'prioritizing' firms that the Council finds to be developing green technologies and socially just labor practices—including worker ownership or codetermination. Socially just and environmentally friendly small firms all over the country—that is, in all twelve of the Fed's Districts—would then benefit. A startup firm developing new air- or water-treatment methods, for example, or perhaps better solar or battery technologies, would be the new paradigms of 'productive' for Fed lending purposes.

If the newly 'spread Fed' limits this revamped facility to financing only such Council-endorsed productive green projects in the Main Street economy rather than speculative gambles in the Wall Street economy, it will both (a) more productively deploy the nation's investment capital and (b) take the wind out of overblown Wall Street sails. And since the Fed Chair will be Co-Chair of the aforementioned Development Council, s/he will have no trouble discerning what has been democratically determined to 'count' as justly and sustainably productive.

Pillar IV: A Universal Digital Savings and Payments Platform

Finally fourth, provide smartphone-accessible digital banking to all citizens, businesses, and legitimate guests of our country. Any American person or business already can open an account with the US Treasury through its TreasuryDirect ('TD') system, out of which one can purchase and into which one can redeem Treasury Securities. All we need to do to convert TreasuryDirect into a socially inclusive universal savings and payments platform is (a) convert TD Accounts into inter-operable P2P digital wallets, and (b) allow digital *dollar* bills—that is, *Federal Reserve* Notes—to be held alongside the *Treasury* Bills and Notes now in those wallets. *Et voila*, no more 'unbanked.'

U.S. Digital Service, an executive agency said to be loved by Vice President Harris, avers it could do the just-mentioned upgrading by summer. In time, we could then migrate the system over to the Fed to integrate into the Fed's broader monetary policy apparatus. Fed 'helicopter drops' or UBI then would be easy. Moreover, all of the green public investing described above in the first three planks of the Plan could be done through these wallets, as could the sending of relief checks, stimulus payments, and more. An NRDC-mandated FFB investment in a new green-tech firm, for example, could be made instantly over the new digital platform. In effect, then, this platform would be the full liability-side counterpart to the asset-side augmentation entailed by the first three Plan-planks just elaborated.

Pillar V: The People's Portfolio

A *Price Stabilization Fund* ('PSF'), a.k.a. *People's Portfolio* will for its part be meant for open market operations to collar what I call *Systemically Important Prices and Indices* (again, 'SIPIs')—housing prices, fuel prices, Libor, some additional staple and commodity prices, and perhaps the SSP or prevailing wage rates at the bottom of the wage scale. I'll cover SIPIS and how to deal with them in much greater detail in Chapter 8, but it will be convenient to afford a preview here so as to show where they'll fit with the once-again Spread Fed in the fuller scheme I envisage.

The basic idea, then, is to recognize that some such prices and indices of such prices are 'systemically important' in the same way as the Systemically Important Financial Institutions ('SIFIs') that FSOC designates. These are prices that pervasively enter either directly into other prices as inputs, or indirectly into other prices by serving as benchmarks or reference points for other pricing decisions or derivative contracts.

The Fed has in effect long recognized at least one species of SIPI, and acted in the capital markets to 'collar' its movements within one narrow band—I refer to prevailing money rental, or 'interest' rates. Recent years have seen the Fed widen the sphere to include mortgage instruments and, now, even broad portfolios of corporate instruments—first in response to the dramas of 2006-09, and more latterly in response to the Covid pandemic.

It is all but inevitable that the Fed, along with a new NRDC, will wish to target more such prices in future in the name of systemic financial stability. That will be partly because of effective credit modulation's practical dependence on good allocation as discussed above, and partly because '*fine-tuning*' will be needed as the nation embarks next year on post-Covid reconstruction and then either a Green New Deal or a 'Building Back Better' revitalization of the kind also discussed above.

We can sum up the results of the foregoing—all five Pillars—in a single diagram as follows, in which connecting lines represent institutional relations and arrows represent financial flows (Fig. A.1).

As noted briefly above, domestic changes of the kind just catalogued, be they in the U.S., elsewhere, or both, will work best under global monetary arrangements that conduce to maximal domestic monetary policy autonomy in every national jurisdiction that participates in the global economy. Happily, as my *Bretton Woods 1.0* and other earlier work, as

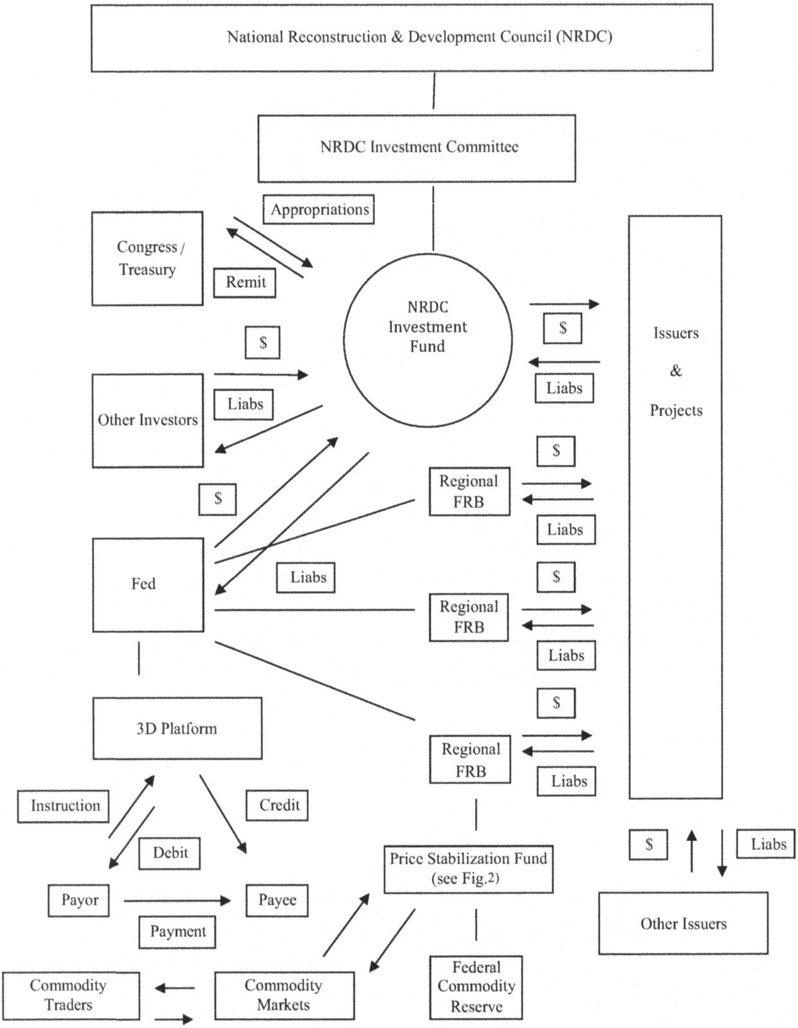

Fig. A.1 Upgraded public finance administrative & financial flow structure

well as my next book, *Global Money*, indicate, we already know how to do this.[1]

All that is required is an updated, digitized rendition of Keynes's International Clearing Union ('ICU') Plan for what ultimately became the International Monetary Fund ('IMF,' 'Fund').

In brief, the plan charges the IMF, still administered by its collaborating member states, with regularly readjusting the exchange rates among national currencies to eliminate and prevent long-term current account imbalances—deficits or surpluses—among trading nation accounts. This the Fund will do via the medium of a bona fide international unit of account, be it Keynes's 'bancor' or the Fund's current 'special drawing rights' ('SDRs'), in relation to which national currencies are valued.

The Fund also will continue to be endowed with issuance authority as at present, though to a quantitatively much greater extent than it possesses at present, in order to smoothen global financial volatility as national central banks do national financial volatility.

My full brief for these reforms notes that the principal obstacle that prevented the Keynes plan's acceptance at Bretton Woods on 1944 is no longer present. At that time, the delegation from the only nation with serious influence—the U.S.—failed to foresee in which the U.S. would incur virtually perpetual current account deficits, while the one delegation that could foresee that because it was experiencing it—that of the U.K.—had virtually no influence thanks to its war-wrought exhaustion.

The present, by contrast, confronts us with a still-dominant power that also has suffered decades-long current account deficits and associated deindustrialization. Hence we now have a globally dominant nation able to appreciate not merely the prospect, but indeed the reality of long-term trade imbalance and consequent productive decline. The present is accordingly the time that Keynes only could dream of—the time when both power and understanding are distributed in a manner conducing to actual implementation of his full ICU plan for the IMF.

****

We began in despair and we end now in hope. A pandemic killed thousands of our own friends, family, and fellow citizens, not to say fellow human beings. Our social and economic fabrics were already, and are still, fraying. Our federal executive for four years, meanwhile, was not *compos mentis*—it was an 'imbecile' executive in precisely the sense Hamilton inveighed against when calling our Constitutional Convention to replace it over 230 years ago[2]—and now appears vulnerable to becoming that way again.

In consequence our states and our cities, which have neither the full territorial jurisdiction nor the currency issuance authority to coordinate and fund fully a true national response to our national crisis, were left to their own sorry devices during the pandemic, and remain jurisdictionally and financially incapable of adequately supporting regional production, development, and economic growth in sustained and inclusive manners. Meanwhile the now rogue Supreme Court appears hell-bent on undoing the past century or more of development of national administrative capacity. It is almost as if the old Anti-Federalists had won, and we're now just as helpless as Hamilton warned we would be if we didn't provide for a competent and duly authorized national executive.[3]

Those at our central bank—our Fed—have seen what is happening, and have in effect said, since 2020, that because states and cities now sometimes must act as our federal administration, they might henceforth be *funded* more like our federal administration—if only Congress so legislates or allows for our central bank. The irony is rich. For what was always the bane of states' rights zealots—a truly centralized central bank and financial system—is the sole instrumentality left to enable our cities and states to preserve and protect themselves, and to fund local businesses that.

But the irony also is double—dare one yet again say 'dialectic'? For to do the job right, the Fed will itself have to 'federate' again, as its opponents made a condition of its very existence and establishment in 1913. It must, that is to say, even while remaining 'central' in centrally monitoring and modulating the nation's free-flowing credit-money supply, re-distribute itself if it would optimally *allocate* that credit-money supply—the nation's primary financial resource.

As I've here argued, that need not be a bad thing. For long after the present crisis has passed, what will be left is a Fed well renewed—a Fed that again is responsive to our towns, cities, states, and their enterprises. It will concern itself not just with hedging and speculation—the business of Wall Street, where only one of its multiple Regional Banks is located—but with *enterprise, production, real wealth, and prosperity.*

That is the business of Main Street, where all of the other Fed Banks are now located. It is the business of *all* of us. It is the business of

America. It will be fully the business of America's *central bank* when, and only when, that bank itself once again looks like America - America in all of its sprawling and federated, big and small, continental republican glory.

Appendix: The National Reconstruction and Continuous Development Act of 2024

Executive Summary

For the past 50 years at least, many American economists and policymakers have erred in their implicit understanding of 'economic development.' Instead of the perpetual process of technological advance and responsive macroeconomic adjustment that it is, development has been conceived as a one-off achievement through which 'underdeveloped' countries become 'developed' countries, then coast on their technical laurels.

Likely stemming as it does from Cold War competition for influence over 'underdeveloped' countries up till the 1990s, this 'takeoff' conception and strategy of economic development, first associated with U.S. Department of State economist Walt Rostow, is ripe for replacement. The present author's InvestAmerica Plan is one such prospective replacement. This proposed bill would for its part now institute the InvestAmerica Plan.

Like the Plan itself, the Bill accordingly aims to work 'big,' transformative changes by levering four surprisingly minimal 'tweaks' to existing federal instrumentalities. These are as follows.

First, the heads of all cabinet-level executive agencies of the U.S. with jurisdiction over primary infrastructures and industries are organized into a strategic development planning body—the National Reconstruction & Development Council ('NRDC'). The Council is charged with developing, regularly updating, and overseeing the implementation of a National Development Strategy ('NDS') analogous to the nation's

R. C. Hockett, *Spread the Fed*,
https://doi.org/10.1007/978-3-031-72051-2

regularly updated National Defense Strategy and Defense Posture Statements formulated by its defense and security agencies. This task includes, among other things, the functions of (a) identifying sectors and Congressional Districts in need of concerted startup assistance, and (b) approving responsive projects, entities, and investment securities as Eligible targets of development investment.

Second, the Federal Financing Bank ('FFB') through which Treasury already funds federal agencies is upgraded with respect to fund inflows and outflows. Inflows will continue to include Congressional appropriations and proceeds of Treasury Securities sales, as presently, but will also include additional public and private sector capital raised through Special Purpose Trusts funding diversified portfolios of Eligible NRDC-designated national development projects. Outflows for their part will continue to include credit-extension and –support afforded to federal agencies, again as at present, but will now also include debt, equity, and hybrid investments in both (a) sub-federal units of government, and (b) private sector firms and consortia of private sector or mixed public-private sector firms designated as Eligible by the NRDC.

Third, the Federal Reserve System is restored to its original role as a network of regional development finance institutions (the Federal Reserve District Banks) overseen and coordinated by an independent executive agency (the Federal Reserve Board of Governors). The Act does this by requiring the Fed to employ its Federal Reserve Act Section 10B, 13, and 14 discounting powers to seek out and afford short- to medium-term liquidity assistance to small businesses designated as Eligible by the NRDC. This form of proactive productive lending, mandated by the text of the Federal Reserve Act itself since 1913 but in recent decades 'honored only in the breach' by the Federal Reserve System, is to replace, where allocative trade-offs have to be made, the speculative lending to secondary and tertiary financial market institutions that the Fed presently favors. Complementary adjustments to the Comptroller of the Currency's bank-chartering and portfolio-regulatory mandates, and to the Federal Deposit Insurance Corporation's capital-regulatory mandate, round out this 'Spread the Fed' pillar of the Plan.

Finally, the Act requires the Department of Treasury to upgrade its present TreasuryDirect system of citizen-accessible Treasury Securities accounts in two ways. First, the U.S. Digital Service is instructed to upgrade TreasuryDirect Accounts into universally available peer-to-peer ('P2P') digital wallets through which Treasury, all citizens, and all approved businesses and guests can transact with each other. And second, the resultant wallets are enabled to receive, hold, and pay out digital Federal Reserve Notes ('dollar bills') in addition to the Treasury Notes, Bills, and Bonds presently authorized to be held. The upshot is a universally accessible digital savings and payments platform that will not only eliminate the problems of commercial and financial exclusion and 'leaky' monetary policy, but also facilitate the efficient and high-velocity operation of those new functions established by the first three pillars of the Plan elaborated above.

The National Reconstruction and Continuous Development Act of 2021

A Bill

To reestablish inclusive, sustainable, and permanently ongoing national, regional, and local economic development as national strategic priorities; to upgrade three existing federal instrumentalities to ensure success in pursuit of this aim; and to provide a universally accessible digital savings and payment platform to all American citizens and businesses in pursuit of the same aim.

Be it enacted by the Senate and House of Representatives of the United States of America in Congress assembled,

Section 1. Short Title.

This Act may be cited as the "National Reconstruction and Continuous Development Act of 2021."

Section 2. Findings and Purpose.

a. Findings.—Congress finds that—

1. For over fifty years, many American economists policy-makers have treated "economic development" as a one-off achievement rather than as a continuous and never-finished process of technical innovation, macroeconomic adaptation, and sustainably inclusive economic growth—as it was viewed for the first two hundred years of the life of our republic;
2. Because of this mistaken understanding of "development" as a one-off achievement rather than a perpetual process, the United States has ceased to employ its primary institutions of public finance, including the Department of the Treasury and the

Federal Reserve System, as institutions of continuous and inclusive National Development in the way that it did until the 1970s;

3. The lost understanding of our institutions of public finance as instrumentalities of continuous economic development has resulted in long-term national underdevelopment—including decades of uninterrupted deindustrialization and infrastructural degradation—of the productive sector's of the nation's economy, along with associated job loss, wage stagnation, impoverishment, private sector indebtedness, extreme economic and racial inequality, and repeated financial market bubbles and busts that destroy real wealth and real lives—dysfunctions that have intensified during the recent Covid pandemic;
4. The lost understanding of our institutions of public finance as instrumentalities of continuous economic development also constitutes a significant national security threat, as (a) rival nations surpass the United States as centers of innovation, progress, production, and growth; and (b) resentments among millions of Americans fuel political disaffection and violent extremism;
5. The lost understanding of our institutions of public finance as instrumentalities of continuous economic development is deeply out of step with the history of our nation and the histories of these institutions and their predecessors, including Treasury Secretary Alexander Hamilton's First Bank of the United States and Society for the Promotion of Useful Manufactures; Treasury Secretary Albert Gallatin's Second Bank of the United States; President Lincoln's Office of the Comptroller of the Currency within the Department of Treasury; the two-tiered Federal Reserve System established on a bipartisan basis in 1913; the War Industries Board and War Finance Corporation established by President Woodrow Wilson; and the War Production Board and Reconstruction Finance Corporation established by Presidents Herbert Hoover and Franklin Roosevelt;
6. Rebuilding the nation's innovative and productive capacities after decades of neglect, as well as restoring continuous and inclusive National Development as strategic national priorities, will require, both for the sake of democratic accountability

and for the sake of project coherence across all Congressional Districts, industries, and infrastructures in the nation, a National Reconstruction and Development Council comprising the Treasury Secretary, the Federal Reserve Chair, and the heads of all Cabinet-level executive agencies with jurisdiction over the nation's primary infrastructures and industries;

7. Rebuilding the nation's innovative and productive capacities after decades of neglect, as well as restoring continuous and inclusive National Development as strategic national priorities, will also be far easier to effectuate, in a manner that also strengthens the Financial Stability of the United States, if the National Reconstruction and Development Council referenced in Subsection (6) immediately above has a financing arm within Treasury like Treasury Secretary Hamilton's First Bank of the United States, Treasury Secretary Gallatin's Second Bank of the United States, President Wilson's War Finance Corporation, and Presidents Hoover's and Roosevelt's Reconstruction Finance Corporation—a role to which the Department of Treasury's already existing Federal Financing Bank, suitably upgraded, is well adapted;
8. Rebuilding the nation's innovative and productive capacities after decades of neglect, as well as restoring continuous and inclusive National Development as strategic national priorities, will also be far easier to effectuate, in a manner that also strengthens the Financial Stability of the United States and fosters new startup industries, small businesses, and National Development across all Congressional Districts of the United States, if the regional Federal Reserve District Banks that constitute the second tier of the Federal Reserve System resume their original mission as a network of regional development finance institutions;
9. Rebuilding the nation's innovative and productive capacities after decades of neglect, as well as restoring continuous and inclusive National Development as strategic national priorities, will also be far easier to effectuate, in a manner that also strengthens the Financial Stability of the individual States and Territories of United States and fosters National Development across all Congressional Districts of the United States, if the

Department of the Treasury upgrades its now universally available system of TreasuryDirect Accounts into a universal digital savings and payments platform available to all Citizens and Businesses of the United States; and

10. Gradually integrating the universal digital savings and payments platform referenced in Subsection (9), immediately above, with the Federal Reserve System's monetary policy apparatus and augmented functionalities as described above and prescribed in this Act, will both (a) render monetary policy more effective and efficient; and (b) enable both the Federal Reserve System and the other instrumentalities mentioned above and upgraded by this Act more effectively and efficiently to discharge the functions described in Subsections (6) through (9) immediately above.

b. Purposes.—The purposes of this Act are—

1. To make the institutional restorations and upgrades referenced in Findings (6) through (10) above, in order—
2. To rectify the deficiencies identified in findings (1) through (5) above.

Section 3. Definitions.

a. Banking Institution.—
b. Community Banking Institution.—
c. Community Development Financial Institution.—
d. Credit Instrument.—
e. Debt Instrument.—
f. Discount.—
g. Discount Window.—
h. Eligible Entity.—
i. Eligible Paper.—
j. Eligible Project.—
k. Equity Instrument.—
l. Hybrid Instrument.—
m. ...

Section 4. National Reconstruction and Development Council.

The following provisions shall take effect within three months of the passage of this Act.—

a. Establishment.— There is established a National Reconstruction and Development Council ("Council," "NRDC") of the United States.
b. Membership and Meetings.— The Council shall consist of the following Members:
    1. Voting Members.—Subject to the joint veto of the Secretary of the Treasury and the Chair of the Federal Reserve Board of Governors, decisions of the Council shall be taken either by consensus or by majority vote of the following Voting Members:
        A. The Secretary of the Treasury, who with the Chair of the Federal Reserve Board of Governors shall serve as Co-Chair of the Council;
        B. The Chair of the Federal Reserve Board of Governors, who with the Secretary of the Treasury shall serve as Co-Chair of the Council;
        C. The Secretary of Agriculture;
        D. The Secretary of Commerce;
        E. The Secretary of Defense;
        F. The Secretary of Energy;
        G. The Secretary of Housing and Urban Development;
        H. The Secretary of the Interior;
        I. The Secretary of Labor;
        J. The Secretary of Transportation;
        K. The Administrator of the Environmental Protection Agency;
        L. The Administrator of the Small Business Administration;
        M. The Director of the Office of Management and Budget;
        N. The U.S. Trade Representative.
    2. Nonvoting Members.—Unless the Voting Members of the Council determine by consensus or by non-vetoed majority decision to exclude them from participation in discussion of certain subjects that implicate national security or confidential supervisory information, the following Nonvoting Members shall serve in advisory capacities as Nonvoting Members of the Council:
        A. The Chief Executive Officer of the Federal Financing Bank as upgraded by Section 5 of this Act.

B. The Chief Financial Officer of the Federal Financing Bank as upgraded by Section 5 of this Act.
C. The Chairs of the Boards and the Presidents of the Regional Federal Reserve District Banks.
D. The Governors of the States and Territories of the United States or their duly appointed Representatives.
E. The Treasurers of the States and Territories of the United States or their duly appointed Representatives.

3. Technical Advisory Committees.—The Council may appoint such Special Advisory, Technical, or Professional Committees as may be useful in carrying out the functions of the Council, including Advisory Committees consisting of State or Multistate Agencies, and the Members of such Committees may be Members of the Council, other persons, or both.
4. Meetings.—
   A. Frequency.— The Council shall meet at the call of either Chairperson or a majority of the Voting Members then serving, but not less frequently than quarterly.
   B. Meeting Procedures.—The Council shall adopt such rules as it may deem necessary for the conduct of the business of the Council. Such rules shall be Rules of Agency Organization, Procedure, or Practice for purposes of Section 553 of Title 5 of the U.S. Code.
   C. Supporting Personnel.—Voting and Nonvoting Members of the Council may be accompanied in Council Meetings by such Supporting Personnel as they require—*provided*, that a majority of Voting Members of the Council do not object, for cause, to their presence.

c. Assistance from other Federal Agencies.— Any Department or Agency of the United States may provide to the Council and any Special Advisory, Technical, or Professional Committee appointed by the Council, such services, funds, facilities, staff, and other support services as the Council may determine advisable.

d. Detail of other Federal Government Employees.— Any Employee of the Federal Government may be Detailed to the Council without separate reimbursement, and such Detail shall be without interruption or loss of civil service status or privilege. An Employee of the Federal Government Detailed to the Council shall report to and be subject to oversight by the Council during the assignment to the

Council, and shall be compensated by the Department or Agency from which the Employee has been Detailed.

e. Purposes and Duties of the Council.—

1. Purposes.—The Purposes of the Council are—
   A. To develop and oversee the implementation of a Cross-Congressional-District and Cross-Sectorally coherent, inclusive, sustainable, and annually updated continuous National Development Strategy ("NDS") for the United States, analogous to the National Defense Strategy and Defense Posture Statements statements regularly updated by the nation's defense and security agencies;
   B. To identify specific Sectors, Regions, and Localities of the National Economy in need of financial and other forms of concerted support in order to realize the aims of the continuous National Development Strategy of the United States;
   C. To designate, in collaboration with the Federal Financing Bank as upgraded pursuant to Section 5 of this Act, Eligible Entities, Eligible Paper, and Eligible Projects in light of the determinations made pursuant to Subsections (A) and (B) immediately above;
   D. To develop, in collaboration with the Federal Financing Bank as upgraded pursuant to Section 5 of this Act, financing mechanisms to provide the Eligible Entity, Eligible Paper, and Eligible Project support referenced in Subsections (B) and (C) immediately above in pursuit of the continuous National Development Strategy referenced in Subsection (A) just above.

Section 5. Federal Financing Bank—Upgraded Functionalities.

Congress shall authorize and instruct the Department of the Treasury to upgrade and supplement the current functionalities of its Federal Financing Bank ('Bank,' 'FFB') in the following manners—

a. Funding Inflows.—With respect to funding inflows, the FFB shall fund its operations not solely through Congressional appropriations made for the Department of Treasury, as presently, but also through issuance of Investment Securities of what ever kinds and in what ever quantities it determines to be useful in drawing private sector investment capital to fund national infrastructure and industrial projects of the kind recommended by the Council; these may include, but shall not be limited to, both FFB Credit Instruments and more Project-Specific Instruments, including Equity, Debt, and Hybrid Instruments, issued by Special Purpose Vehicles (SPVs) associated with particular Project Portfolios; Section 9(a) of the Federal Financing Bank Act of 1973, Public Law 93–224, is accordingly amended as follows: between the present first and second sentences is interpolated the sentence, "The Bank is also authorized, with the approval of the Secretary of the Treasury, to settle and manage Special Purpose Trusts, such Trusts to hold portfolios of Eligible Paper issued by Eligible Entities in connection with Eligible Projects, and to be funded through issuance of such Debt, Equity, or Hybrid Investment Securities as the Bank shall deem prudent, as consistent with Subsection (c) of this Section ("Public Control") below.

b. Funding Outflows.—With respect to funding outflows, the FFB shall extend financial support to Eligible Projects recommended by the Council not only in the form of credit or credit-support, as it does now, but also through the purchase of such Eligible Paper, including Debt, Equity, and Hybrid Financial Instruments, of what ever kinds and in what ever quantities it determines to be useful in fostering the construction of new infrastructures and industries deemed in need of such fostering by the Council, including with a view to catalyzing supplementary private financing to the same; the FFB shall also be authorized to extend credit not only to federal instrumentalities, as it is now, but also to state, local, regional, and such other sub-federal units of government and Eligible Entities as the Council determines to be in need of such funding; Section 6(a) of the Federal Financing Bank Act of 1973, Public Law 93–224, is accordingly amended as follows: both occurrences of the phrase "Federal agency" to be deleted and replaced by the phrase "Eligible Entity."

c. Public Control.—In its expanded functionalities in respect of both inflows and outflows of funds as described in Subsections (a) and (b) immediately above, the FFB will retain the right of ultimate disposition of the funds it receives for investment and the funds it invests, permitting no private sector investor or manager anything more than an advisory role as to the disposition of FFB-received and –managed funds.

Section 6. Productive Federal Reserve and National Bank Lending. Congress shall authorize and instruct the Board of Governors of the Federal Reserve System, the Office of the Comptroller of the Currency within the Department of Treasury, and the Federal Deposit Insurance Corporation to upgrade their current operations in the following manners—

a. Federal Reserve Discounting.—The twelve Regional Federal Reserve District Banks shall affirmatively seek, in collaboration with the Comptroller of the Currency, and with Banking, Community Banking, and Community Development Financial Institutions where possible, Eligible Projects deemed desirable by the Council that are in need of short-term (up to 24 months) funding; Eligible Paper may be discounted directly under the Federal Reserve Act Section 14 authority, or indirectly via Member Banks acting under the Federal Reserve Act Section 10B or Section 14 authority—*provided*, that all other 'safety and soundness' criteria imposed in the conduct of Section 10B or 14 Discounting shall continue to be imposed; Section 10B(a) of the Federal Reserve Act, Public Law 63–43, is accordingly amended as follows: delete 'four' and insert 'twenty-four'; Section 13(2) of the Federal Reserve Act, Public Law 63–43, is also amended as follows: in the final sentence, delete '90 days' and insert 'twenty-four months'; and Section 14(2)(b)(1) of the Federal Reserve Act, Public Law 63–43, is amended as follows: delete 'six' and insert 'twenty-four';
b. Comptroller Chartering and Portfolio Regulation.—The Office of the Comptroller of the Currency ('Comptroller,' 'OCC') shall affirmatively include determinations made by the Council as to the productive needs of the nation both in exercising its discretion in conferring National Association banking charters upon prospective Banking Institutions and in regulating National Associations' asset portfolios—*provided*, that all other 'safety and soundness' criteria imposed in the conduct of these regulatory tasks shall continue to be imposed; 12 U.S.C. § 1816(6) is accordingly amended as follows: after the first sentence, insert the sentence "'Convenience and needs'

is to be understood first by reference to 'Eligible Projects' as defined or designated by the National Reconstruction and Development Council."; the Comptroller is also instructed to amend 12 C.F.R. § 5.20(e)(ii)(B) as follows: after the word "served," insert: ", with 'necessity' to be understood first by reference to 'Eligible Projects' as defined or designated by the National Reconstruction and Development Council."; the Comptroller is also instructed to amend 12 C.F.R. § 1.2(m) as follows: after Subsection (3), insert "(4) an investment security issued to finance an 'Eligible Project' as defined or designated by the National Reconstruction and Development Council.";

c. Federal Deposit Insurance Corporation Capital Regulation.— The Federal Deposit Insurance Corporation ("Corporation," "FDIC") shall include determinations made by the Council as to the productive needs of the nation in regulating the leverage employed by all Insured Depository Institutions, in particular, by risk-weighting credit extended by said Institutions to projects deemed desirable by the Council at seventy-five (75) *per centum* of face value—*provided*, that all other "safety and soundness" criteria imposed in the conduct of this regulatory task shall continue to be imposed; the Corporation is accordingly instructed to amend 12 C.F.R. § 3.32(l) as follows: after Subsection (6), insert "(7) a national bank or Federal savings association must assign a 75 percent risk weight to an exposure to an Eligible Project as defined or designated by the National Reconstruction and Development Council."

Section 7. Digital Treasury Direct Wallets.

Congress authorizes and instructs the Department of the Treasury as follows—

a. Digital P2P TreasuryDirect Wallets.—The Department of the Treasury shall upgrade its existing system of TreasuryDirect Accounts as follows—

1. Digital Account Wallets.—The Department of Treasury shall, with all deliberate speed—

A. Add peer-to-peer ("P2P") Digital Wallet Interoperability to all TreasuryDirect Accounts, enabling all Wallet Holders to transact directly in real time with one another, such that Wallet

Holders without Savings or Transaction Accounts held with other institutions, including Banking Institutions and Thrift Organizations, may transact directly with one another through TreasuryDirect Wallets as readily as they can transact with Treasury itself;

B. Cryptographically build into the TreasuryDirect Wallet system all privacy protections that TreasuryDirect Accounts currently offer or that Banking Institutions are now or in future shall be required by law to provide, which ever is the more secure;

C. Retain the services of U.S. Digital Service ("USDS") to perform the upgrades prescribed in Subsections (A) and (B) immediately above;

2. Dollar Holdings.—All holders of TreasuryDirect Accounts and Account Wallets shall be authorized and enabled to hold Federal Reserve instruments—in particular, Federal Reserve Notes ("dollar bills") and their digital equivalent—in their TreasuryDirect Accounts and Account Wallets on equal terms to those on which they hold Treasury Notes, Treasury Bills, Treasury Bonds, and such other Treasury instruments as the Treasury issues and enables to be held in TreasuryDirect Accounts;

3. Bank Account Interoperability.— All TreasuryDirect Accounts shall retain such interoperability with Bank Transaction Accounts as they currently have, and shall also be made accessible, through appropriate OCC and FDIC rulemaking, without payment of fees through all teller windows and Automatic Teller Machines ("ATMs") operated by National Associations and all other Federally Insured Depository Institutions;

b. Shared Federal Reserve Administration.—The Department of

Treasury and the Federal Reserve Board of Governors shall collaborate to enable migration of the system of TreasuryDirect Wallets either to Federal Reserve administration or to joint Treasury and Federal Reserve administration as soon as is reasonably possible, with a view to enabling full integration into both (a) the Federal Reserve System's monetary policy apparatus, and (b) the FFB's and Federal Reserve System's upgraded functions as prescribed in Section 6 of this Act immediately above; Treasury in consultation with the Federal Reserve Board of

Governors may, within its discretion, limit maximum dollar holdings in TreasuryDirect wallets if necessary to maintain the monetary policy efficacy of the Federal Reserve System—*provided*, that no such limit shall be set beneath $2000.

Notes

1. See Hockett, sources cited supra Chapter 3, note 27. Also Hockett, Global Money (manuscript under review, 2024).
2. See again Hockett, sources cited supra Part I, note 2.
3. Id.

Index

R. C. Hockett, *Spread the Fed*,
https://doi.org/10.1007/978-3-031-72051-2

The manufacturer's authorised representative in the EU is Springer
Nature Customer Service Centre GmbH, Europaplatz 3, 69115 Heidelberg,
Germany. If you have any concerns regarding our products, please
contact ProductSafety@springernature.com

Printed and bound by CPI Group (UK) Ltd, Croydon, CR0 4YY
01/10/2026
02225953-0001